Sacrificial Offerings

Monologues of Real Women in History & Religion

Coralie Cederna Johnson

Sacrificial Offerings

Published by:
Wildwood Press
www.wildwoodpress.org
and
Coralie Cederna Johnson
cjohnson@umich.edu

ISBN 10-0615857655
ISBN 13-978-0-615-85765-7

Women/Religion/Drama

Cover Design by Dr. Paul J. Jacobs
Cover Photo by Coralie Cederna Johnson

Printed in the United States of America

Acknowledgements

Eastern Michigan University Masters Committee:
Dr. Margot Duley
Dr. Laura George
Dr. Kerry Graves

Cover Design:
Dr. Paul J. Jacobs

Author Photo:
Ben F. Sayer & Carrie Jay Sayer

Masters Program Performance 2000
EMU Quirk Theater
Cast:
Chris Evans
Carrie Jay Sayer
Brenda Pilgrim
Sandy DiCesare
Julianne Dolan
Marty Smith

Women's History Month Performance 2001
EMU Quirk Theater
Cast:
Chris Evans
Carrie Jay Sayer
Brenda Pilgrim
Sandy DiCesare
Julianne Dolan
Dr. Jeffrey L. Duncan

Readers:
Dr. Lorraine Grinnell, Cindy Parker, Jim Johnson

A Note from the Author

Sacrificial Offerings: The play presents the riveting monologues of twenty-four remarkable women in history...women who refused to be silenced. As their stories come to life, through staged performances or silent reading, we learn how they changed the world through religious leadership, acts of courage, and martyrdom. We witness their boundless capacity for love, faith, and hope. And we encounter the profound strength and amazing spirit of women through time:

Visionaries who pioneered pathways for women to follow and choose religious freedom.

Victims who were persecuted for religious beliefs or charged with crimes such as witchcraft and using magical powers.

Victors who defied physical danger and dedicated their lives to powerful personal missions.

The life stories of these courageous women stand as historical proof that determined females can successfully challenge and change patriarchal religious, political, and societal beliefs and boundaries.

Reflections on Women and Religion: This body of work offers glimpses into the lives of women of faith and their visions of spirituality, devotion, and divine love. Their words provide powerful inspiration as they share their dedication to judgment-free living, listening, learning, and loving.

Coralie Cederna Johnson

About the Author

Coralie Cederna Johnson

Coralie is an author, a playwright, and a teacher of Women and Gender Studies at Eastern Michigan University, Ypsilanti, MI. She holds a Bachelor of Arts in Human Resource Management from Concordia University and a Masters in Women's Studies from EMU. She wrote, directed, and produced *Sacrificial Offerings* for her Masters Project and the play was presented in EMU's Quirk Theater. It was also performed for Women's History Month 2002.

Her plays have been produced on professional stages: *Pigeons in the Park* at Performance Network, Ann Arbor, MI and *BEES* at Boarshead Theater, Lansing, MI. She is currently at work on a new play, *The Red Dress Diaries*, a collection of monologues for and about women, which include pivotal moments in the lives of women as they deal with issues such as eating disorders, homophobia, racism, acts of violence including bullying, sexual abuse, and rape.

Coralie is the author of two books, *The Wishing Years* and *A Tree Grows in Trout Creek*, available from Wildwood Press or from the author: cjohnson@umich.edu.

Contents

The Play ~ Sacrificial Offerings

Reflections on Women & Religion

The Women of Sacrificial Offerings

BISHOP, BRIDGET (1632~1692)
(Bridget Bishop was the first of several innocent women to be accused of witchcraft, found guilty and hanged during the Salem Witch Trials of 1692.)

BOSANQUET-FLETCHER, MARY (1739~1815)
(Raised in a wealthy Roman Catholic home, Mary Fletcher embraced Methodism and became one of its first female preachers.)

LUTHER, KATHARINA (1499~1555)
(Katharina Von Bora broke her vows of monasticism and left the Catholic Church, after being inspired by the writings of the Reverend Martin Luther also a former monastic. In 1523, she left the Cistercian Convent in Nimbschen, Germany and later married Luther.)

BROWN, OLYMPIA (1835~1926)
(Born in a log cabin in Prairie Ronde, Michigan—Cass County—in 1835, Olympia Brown became the first American woman to be formally ordained as a fully authoritative minister of the Universalist Church. She later left the ministry to work for women's suffrage.)

WESLEY, SUSANNA (1669~1742)
(Susanna Wesley was the twenty-fifth child of Samuel and Susanna Annesley. She is often called the Mother of Methodism because her sons John and Charles founded the Methodist religion.)

<u>BESANT, ANNIE</u> (1847~1933)
(Annie Besant, once married to a minister, became disillusioned with Christianity in the 1880's because of its oppression of women. A freethinker, she turned to atheism and later to Theosophy and Spiritualism.)

<u>HOSOKAWA, GRACIA</u> (1563~1600)
(Lady Hosokawa Gracia was born into one of the greatest samurai families in Japan in the Sixteenth Century. Though she converted to Christianity, she used her Zen Buddhist philosophy and beliefs to interpret the teachings of the Jesuits.)

<u>JUDSON, ANN HASSELTINE</u> (1789~1826)
(Ann Judson was the first American woman to travel overseas to do missionary work.)

<u>CLITHEROW, MARGARET</u> (1556~1586)
(In Sixteenth Century England, it was against the law to be Catholic. If one did not attend Protestant services at the Church of England, it was considered an act of treason against the government. Margaret Clitherow, who secretly provided food, shelter and a place to say Mass for Catholic priests, served several prison terms for these crimes. On Lady Day, now known as Good Friday, 1586, she was pressed to death for her religious beliefs.)

<u>WILKINSON, JEMIMA</u> (1752~1819)
(Raised in a Rhode Island Quaker home, Jemima Wilkinson, later joined the New Light Baptists and, in 1776, became the first American woman to form a religious group, called The Universal Friends.)

MURRAY, GRACE (1738~1803)
(Grace Murray was one of a few women who worked with John Wesley and became a leader within the early Methodist movement. In the late Eighteenth Century, Wesley, who was in love with her, asked her to marry him.)

DUCHESNE, ROSE PHILIPPINE (1769~1852)
(Rose Duchesne's lifelong dream was to work with the Native American Indians.)

LAVEAU, MARIE (1794~1881)
(Marie Laveau practiced both Voodoo and Catholicism in early Nineteenth Century New Orleans. She used her knowledge of sorcery and Black Magic to both obtain personal power and to help the poor and the sick.)

AYLWARD, GLADYS (1904~1970)
(When the China Inland Mission Center of London turned Gladys Aylward down for missionary work in China, she saved the money she earned as a parlor maid until she had enough for her passage. In 1930, she arrived in a small mountain town, Shansi, just south of Peking (Beijing) eager to spread the word of the Christian Bible.)

TEKAKWITHA, KATERI (1656~1680)
(Kateri Tekakwitha, born in 1656, defied her Mohawk tribe by refusing to marry and instead choosing to embark on a life of virginal devotion to the Christian God. Disfigured and almost blinded by smallpox, Kateri became known as the "Lily of the Mohawks" when, immediately upon her death, all traces of her deformities vanished.)

WILLARD, FRANCES (1839~1898)

(An 1880's educator and suffragist, Frances Willard's concern for the social status of women led her to activism for the Women's Christian Temperance Union. She believed that women could achieve political authority through the Temperance Movement.)

JONAS, REGINA (1902~1944)

(Regina Jonas, born in Berlin, Germany in 1902, graduated from the Academy for the Science of Judaism as a teacher of religion, and was the first woman to be ordained a rabbi.)

SNOW, ELIZA (1804~1887)

(In the early 1800's, Eliza Snow's family left their Baptist faith to join the Mormon community in Nauvoo, Illinois.)

LEE, ANN (1736~1784)

(Born in Manchester, England to a working class family, Ann Lee married at a young age and gave birth to four children. All four were either stillborn or died shortly after birth. Through a vision, she came to believe that she was the female Christ and from this revelation went on to form the Shaker religion.)

DYER, MARY BARRETT (1614~1660)

(Mary Dyer gave her life on the gallows to free her fellow Quakers from religious persecution. After her death, Charles II, King of England forbade all further killings of Quakers in Boston.)

<u>SETON, ELIZABETH</u> (1774~1821)
(Elizabeth Ann Seton, widowed mother of five children, founded the Sisters of Charity and Roman Catholic parochial education in the United States.)

<u>McPHERSON, AIMEE SEMPLE</u> (1890~1944)
(Aimee Semple McPherson, evangelist and faith healer, was a woman of great determination who, with her mother, built a 5,000-seat Temple in which to do her personal preaching.)

<u>CROSBY, FRANCES JANE</u> (1820~1915)
(Accidentally blinded by an unlicensed country doctor, who incorrectly applied hot mustard poultices to her eyes at the age of six weeks, Fanny Crosby went on to write over five thousand inspirational hymns of Christian praise.)

<u>BLAVATSKY, HELENA</u> (1831~1891)
(Helena Petrovna Blavatsky was the founder of the Theosophical Society, a worldwide association dedicated to the belief that there is one Divine Spirit to which all people are universally connected.)

Sacrificial Offerings

Coralie Cederna Johnson

The Setting

There is an altar down right. Six chairs are set at left center in a circular pattern and facing upstage. To the right of the altar is a pulpit. Down left is a box filled with the sacrificial offerings (props).

Fanny Crosby's hymn, Blessed Assurance, plays in the background as six women in black file in and sit in the chairs. A man enters and goes to the pulpit, where he stands watching the women.

To deliver her monologue, each woman rises, collects her prop from the box and walks toward the audience. She chooses a spot downstage (this spot should vary with different women) and tells her story. When she is through speaking, she will walk down right and place her offering on the altar. She will then return to her chair and continue to face upstage.

During each monologue, the man stands in his pulpit and continues watching the women. When the last woman, Madame Blavatsky, completes her last line, "They are…as brilliant stars among the planets shining in perpetual hope…an example for us all to follow," the women stand, turn, and proceed downstage where they join together to say their final lines.

Bridget Bishop (1632~1692)

(Bridget Bishop was the first of several innocent women to be accused of witchcraft, found guilty, and hanged during the Salem Witch Trials of 1692.)

MAN:

The spirit of joy shall reign in the hearts of women who are gentle of thought, who honor, obey, and have faith. Faith is the key to everlasting happiness. Believe and all that is heavenly shall be yours. Believe and you shall be saved...

BRIDGET:

(Removes paring knife from the box of offerings.)

I were sitting in my kitchen peeling carrots, cutting them up with my carving knife, when they come by. I never even heard them coming. They just walked right into my house and stood there—leering.

"We come to get you Bridget Bishop, 'cause you been causing fits upon many innocent young girls."

It were a great fright that come over mee. It were like fiery coals got in my blood and spurted up inside my skull. It made mee think to run. But a great numbness fell upon my ankles and my knees and I could not move. And...and my tongue got tied. And I could barely get words off it.

"Who says I done this?" I ask them.

And they say to mee, it were Edward my husband himself who tould them, "The devil come unto her and take over her body and shee let him."

I feel the carrot I were cutting getting squashed, until it goes all wet and slimy in my hands. Accused I were of being a devil's witch, and by my own husband's claim. As for the others...it were, most of all, loose-tongued liars who said I caused the fits.

And it were Shattuck, the town dyer, who tould them, "Bridget Bishop are tainted by the devil's touch. Shee have business to do with Spirits. Shee sneaks to my house and leaves mee lace to dye. Red! Then wears it like a blaze of glory on her dress."

While they watched and hovered, I put the carrots in water, rinsed the knife, and put on my blackest cap and cape. Then they tied my wrists with prickly rope, took mee to the town jail, and locked mee up.

This Evil Spell come unto mee on a dark day in Salem, Massachusetts in the year of 1692. But, I remained a member of Mr. Hale's Church...and...even up to the last, a member in good standing!

I tould them over and over, I were innocent. I tould them I don't know the devil. I never met him. And I don't know where he is. But eight days later, I were the first. And those what followed, their minds were tortured worse. For, by that time, everyone knew what lay ahead.

(Places knife, her offering, on altar.)

Mary Bosanquet-Fletcher (1739~1815)

(Raised in a Roman Catholic home, Mary Fletcher embraced Methodism and became one of its first female preachers.)

MAN:

For those who are righteous, there is no death. Believe in all that is virtuous and you shall be spared the agonies of hell. But, above all, women, remember that obedience is the measure of the purity of soul...

MARY:

(Removes Methodist materials from box.)

My family, the Bosanquet's, had always cherished their faith. No Bosanquet had ever left the Roman Catholic religion. So you can imagine the distress of my parents, upon discovering that I had been given Methodist materials...and by one of their maidservants. It was a terrible scene! They banished me to my bedchambers and promptly dismissed the servant. "Wayward," they called her.

It was never my intention to cause such a chaotic situation. But I was a curious child, anxious to learn about life outside my home, eager to know more about the interpretations of scripture. When the illegal literature was discovered, I was forced to give it up and forbidden to continue any future exploration. But I had already read the materials, become captivated by the new teachings and committed them to heart. I knew that, as soon as I was old enough to leave Leytonstone, I would go to London to learn more about the fascinating new Methodist movement.

My great desire to study the scriptures, my gift for oratory, my determination to let nothing stand in my way of discovering new knowledge—all of these things were deeply ingrained in my personality from a young age and continued to guide me along life's path.

Subsequently—and this will likely come as no surprise to any of you—when I grew to adulthood and was told that women could not and should not take the pulpit, I demanded to know why not. I put the question directly, and repeatedly, to John Wesley. But, while I awaited his response, I did not sit idly by. Oh no, I made myself quite busy...teaching scriptures at the weekly Methodist Society Meetings. When finally John conceded that perhaps God might even consider women for His work, I was, shall we say, more than ready.

(Places Methodist materials on altar.)

Katharina Luther (1499 ~ 1555)

(Katharina Von Bora broke her vows of monasticism and left the Catholic Church after being inspired by the writings of the Reverend Martin Luther also a former monastic. In 1523, she left the Cistercian convent in Nimbschen, Germany and later married Luther.)

MAN:

The voices of the disobedient must be quelled. Let them find joy in silence. Blessed are the women who seek monasticism, who pray in silent thought, whose hearts are filled with soundless speech...

KATHARINA:

(Takes rosary from pocket.)

There were eleven of us...quiet women hidden away from the world, sheltered from everyday life, living in a place many of us had not ourselves chosen...conditioned to a world of cloistered prayer, reading, and the work of the nunnery...

There were eleven of us...quiet women who curiously read the words of Martin Luther, who dared to break the vows of silence, who humbly questioned the teachings of the church...celibacy...monastic vows...

There were eleven of us...quiet women who soundlessly planned our escape, whose lives depended upon our stealth, whose actions were punishable by nothing less than death...

There were eleven of us...quiet women whose frightened hearts beat a deafening roar as we awaited Merchant Kopp's fish wagon, who crawled indelicately into his empty fish barrels, who weathered the whip and thrash of the wagon as we made our way to Wittenberg...

There were eleven of us...quiet women, who burst beyond the confines of our convent walls and escaped captivity...

There were eleven of us…once quiet women, whose lives were spared that suffocating state of still and absolute silence, whose voices raised on high, sang out in grateful praise!

(Places rosary on altar.)

Olympia Brown (1835~1926)

(Born in Prairie Ronde, Michigan, Olympia Brown became the first American woman to be ordained a minister of the Universalist Church.)

MAN:

Women must be obedient. If they refuse, the gentle strap of justice shall be used to smite their sins of prideful declaration. Women's silence is their testament to duty and to love...

OLYMPIA:

(Removes prayer book, with ballot inside, from box.)

Women, let me warn you, men will try to still your voices. Do not let them! Your dreams and goals are your own. And just because you were born female, does not mean you must give them up. Not to sound arrogant, but I certainly never gave up on mine, although there were times when...well, it was difficult. I was a teacher at age fifteen. But I wanted more. I wanted to not just preach in the pulpit, but also be a full-fledged minister with all the rights of ordination. I wanted an education equal to that of men.

The University of Michigan turned me away, because I was female. But Mount Holyoke College allowed me entrance. From there, I gained admittance to Antioch College. But when I searched for a divinity school, I found there were only three schools in the United States that accepted women. St. Lawrence Seminary was one of these and very unwillingly—and with great trepidation—they permitted me to enroll. There I received my theological education. But no woman had ever been ordained in full denominational authority, so you can imagine the troublesome times with which I was faced. Still I would not back down! I was ordained a Universalist minister in June 1863 and, following this, held full pastorates in several United States cities.

But, when in 1886, I met Susan B. Anthony, I turned in my pastorate to work for the American Equal Rights Association. I never once thought that we would not win the vote, although it was a long and arduous fight. Of my closest friends and fellow suffragettes—Susan B. Anthony,

Lucy Stone, Elizabeth Cady Stanton, Matilda Joslyn Gage—I was the only one who lived long enough to see the 19th Amendment to the Constitution of the United States passed. I was the only one who lived long enough to cast my vote.

(Waves ballot in air.)

Women, let me warn you, men will try to still your voices. Do not let them!

(Places book and ballot on altar.)

Susanna Wesley (1669~1742)

(Susanna Wesley was the twenty-fifth child of Samuel and Susanna Annesley. She is often called the Mother of Methodism because her sons John and Charles founded the Methodist religion

MAN:

A woman's place is in the home, for there she will be honored for her contributions as the fruitful bearer of life. She will be anointed and celebrated for the sons she will bear to man...

SUSANNA:

(Removes Bible from box.)

The Lord entrusted me with the souls of nineteen children. Ten of the nineteen lived past infancy. The most famous of my children were John and Charles, who, as you most likely are aware, created the Methodist religion. But it could have been any of my children, who struck out against the church as we knew it. It could have been Sukey or Anne or Mary or Emilia, if times had been different, for I showed no partiality in saving the souls of either my sons or my daughters. All of God's souls were equally important to Him and to me.

I provided guidance for the souls of my sons and daughters through organization, discipline, and education. Many families did not understand these three ingredients were fundamental to freeing their children—both male and female children—from false and dangerous information. Having been blessed with my own parents, who through the mercy and goodness of God, understood that no soul should go untaught, I gained the wisdom and knowledge to instruct my children at home. Each child received instruction as part of the family group and individually as well. Each evening of the week was dedicated to a particular person for interview and discussion. I did the best I could with each—male or female —for I believe: The Lord careth not if the soul He sends to earth is inhabited in the body of a female or a male. He careth only if that soul returneth to His heavenly fold.

(Places Bible on altar.)

Annie Besant (1847~1933)

(Annie Besant, once married to a Christian minister, turned to atheism and later to Theosophy and spiritualism.)

MAN:

Women are to be cherished and loved for their beauty. They are the flowers that bloom in splendid shining color. They are a joy for their husbands to behold...

ANNIE:

(Removes book from box.)

Obscene libel they called it! *The Laws of Population*, my book promoting birth control. But prison was nothing compared with the suffering of women who were repeatedly bound to service their husbands' needs, only to find they were again with child. Many had barely recovered from childbirth when they found themselves pregnant again. The cycle was vicious: birth...service...birth...illness...breasts drying...children hungry...starving...death...

Women bleeding, dying from secret attempts to rid their bodies of the forming parasites within. Who could believe in a god who visited death and illness upon unsuspecting women?

And who was I to stay silent about the terrible abuses of women? For my transgressions in criticizing Christianity, my husband, the good minister, banned me from my home. Put me out on the streets. Took custody of my children. Still, as torturous as was my own personal loss, I knew that I had to give breath to the tragic voices of women, their enslavement in abject poverty, pain, privation. Who would do it, if not I?

Wrenched from my children and flung into a new phase of freedom, I enrolled at London University, where I earned a degree in science. Shortly afterward I met the marvelous spiritualist Madame Blavatsky, who introduced me to the foundations of Theosophy: reincarnation, the oneness of religion, a divine spirit, a universal approach to social and political problems of the world. All of this made good sense for my public beliefs and work for women—including the right for females to vote!

It seems that everything in life eventually comes full circle. I still do not know if there is a divine spirit, one who grants women their most sought after wishes. But I do know that, after I moved to India to study Hinduism, I was reunited with my children, when both my daughter and my son came to live with me. I suppose one could entertain the thought that all my wishful yearning had risen up to a higher place...a place in which the spirit of One Divine Being heard and chose to answer my request...I suppose one could...

(Places book on altar.)

Gracia Hosokawa (1563~1600)

(Lady Hosokawa Gracia was born into one of the greatest samurai families in Japan in the Sixteenth Century. Though she converted to Christianity, she used her Zen Buddhist philosophy and beliefs to interpret the teachings of the Jesuits.)

MAN:

Women must keep their thoughts pure and chaste. It is the way to simple devotion. In times of trouble and strife, let the good wife give up her hopes and dreams for the sake of her loved ones…

GRACIA:

Had I been born a man-child, I would have taken up the Samurai sword and fought alongside my father, the general Matshuhide Akechi. But I was not born a man-child. At birth I was named Tamako, *jewel-child*, and my life took a different turn. Instead, I was named the daughter of a traitor, when my father assassinated General Oda to prevent him from taking over the Shogunate in Japan.

By this time I was a young married woman. And, in order to safeguard my husband and children from harm, I laid down my heart at my husband's feet and begged him to divorce me, which he had the wisdom to do, despite the love we shared…

(Removes "Japanese/Catholic" icon from box.)

I joined my Buddhist beliefs to the Christian way and received my baptismal name, Grace—Gracia—from the missionaries.

At one time, not long before the Warring Years took place—a few centuries—when Kyoto Imperial Court governed Japanese society, women were held in high esteem equal to men. The written word of women was met with respect. Property could be owned by them. Their written words were honored. But that had been long before my day.

Had I been born a man-child, I would have lived as a defending champion of the Imperial Court. I would likely not have been taken hostage in my own home, as were the many wives of men who served. I would have had some control over my destiny.

I tell you none of this with regret...only as a memory of how life might have been, if I had not been born a woman-child, a jewel-child.

(Places icon on altar.)

Ann Hasseltine Judson (1789~1826)

(Ann Judson was the first American woman to travel overseas to do missionary work.)

MAN:

Let her follow her husband down the path of righteousness. Let her learn that she is ever his helpmate. In times of helplessness, let her go to him and plead for mercy…

ANN:

(Removes framed wedding portrait from box.)

I know that many of my friends thought me a romantic adventurer, when I agreed to marry Adoniram and cross the seas with him to India. But what they didn't know is that I had already dedicated my life to God's work, well before I met him.

We set sail in February 1812, just one week after our wedding. I can see us still, as if it were just yesterday, standing on the deck of the ship, waving to our families and friends, watching their figures becoming smaller and smaller…then disappear as we swept slowly out to sea.

The journey was brutal and seemingly endless. But after four months of travel and ceaseless bouts of severe seasickness, we finally arrived at our destination. Our relief, however, was momentary for we directly discovered we were neither welcome to stay nor to sow our Christian beliefs in Calcutta. In fact, before we were even able to unpack, explicit orders were issued by the government that we must leave the country immediately or suffer severe consequences.

We escaped to Burma where—even though the threat of war between the British and the Burman's seemed imminent—we were able to begin our work. Adoniram poured over his books, carefully studying the written word, attempting to perfect his use of the Burmese language. While I, on the other hand, through the giving of household instructions to the natives, found a way to learn—straight away—the spoken word. Though we frequently used our own unique methods to accomplish similar goals, we generally reached the same conclusion. And that was one of the things that was so special about our marriage. We always maintained respect for each other's individual efforts.

(Places portrait on altar.)

Perhaps my friends were right. Perhaps I was a romantic adventurer. For there was not a single day that passed in which I did not awake and rise with an eager spirit of anticipation for what challenges the new dawn might bring. Whatever they were to be, I knew that Adoniram and I would meet them head-on and purposefully—together. For, unlike many marriages of our day, ours was a partnership of body, mind, and heart, a union of two souls bent in the same direction, an equal force to be reckoned with.

Margaret Clitherow (1556~1586)

(In sixteenth century England, it was against the law to be Catholic. If one did not attend protestant services at the Church of England, it was considered an act of treason against the government. Margaret Clitherow, who secretly provided food and shelter and a place to say Mass for Catholic priests, served several prison terms for these crimes. On Lady Day, now known as Good Friday, 1586, she was pressed to death for her religious beliefs.)

MAN:

Pray for guidance in fulfilling your Godly roles. You are the honored of the sexes. Give gratitude to men for your respite from war...

MARGARET:

(Removes ornate crucifix from box.)

"Confess your crimes!" they demanded, when I was brought before the Council of the North in York and stood accused of harboring priests. "Confess!"

Many said I could have prevented my own suffering just by speaking out...but...

A woman does not enter motherhood immediately knowing how to care for her child. Yet—and this is a strange and wonderful gift from God—as swiftly as the pains of childbirth recede and the newly born infant is placed at her breast does a woman know that she will protect her innocent from any and all harm. A mother makes many choices for her children, some of which are simple, others of which are severe. But, in all things, a mother protects. Sometimes she must sound out with the voice of a trumpet. Sometimes she must choose silence.

Yes, many said I could have prevented my own suffering just by speaking out...but...none of them were the mother of my innocent children.

The choice was really one of the simple ones. I bid no words pass my lips. I bound myself to silence. I pled neither guilty, nor not guilty. You see, the only witnesses to my crimes were my own small children. I could not allow them to be questioned, to turn me in by telling the truth, to live with the guilt of knowing they had sealed my fate.

(Places crucifix on altar.)

Jemima Wilkinson (1752~1819)

(Raised in a Quaker home, Jemima Wilkinson later joined the New Light Baptists. And, in 1776, became the first American woman to form a religious group, called The Universal Friends.)

MAN:

It is the immortal plan that men shall lead the world in faith. Women, do not dabble in religious pretext. Illness and contempt will be delivered upon those who disregard these words. And they shall be stoned…

JEMIMA:

I was returning from worship, a most satisfying service at the New Light Baptist Church. Rousing, you know. Nothing like the Quaker meetings of my youth. It was autumn 1776. And as I hurried toward home, leaves, dead and dying, attached themselves to the hem of my skirts. Crushed under the burden of my boots, they trailed along, clinging like fragile parasites.

I felt the first wave of indisposition sweep over me, just as I turned the knob and stepped inside. Never a sickly woman, I endeavored to ignore these early signs of illness. But when I fell faint upon attempting to leave my bed the next morning, I knew the ailment, with which I had become afflicted, was of a most serious nature. I did not understand then, however, that it was to be a potentially fatal fever. Boiling hot sweat, then chills cold as ice wracked my body, twisting and turning it in pain. And, when I could bear my burden no longer, I heard my voice cry out, "Let death console!"

More simply than I could ever have imagined, I slipped away from that writhing useless body. The color of night, like a velvet cloak, pressed in upon me. And then...and then...I found myself adrift in a corridor of darkness. But I saw a light, a single ray of brilliant beaming light in the far off distance. AND I BECAME ONE WITH GOD! I became that light—the light of the world. And I was SAVED!

From that day forward, upon my return to that earthly dwelling place called home, I could foretell the future. And for this...

(Takes stone from pocket.)

for this, I was stoned! Quaker and Baptist alike expelled me from their presence. But, knowing that nothing must stand in the way of my God-given mission, I used the gift of clairvoyance I had received, along with the Light, as a beacon of truth for sinners. Sinners trudging in this world of fleshly charms. Sinners who, as disciples of the Universal Publik Friends, could find redemption. Sinners who, like me, could be SAVED.

(Places stone on altar.)

Grace Murray (1738~1803)

(Grace Murray was one of a few women who worked with John Wesley and became a leader within the early Methodist movement. In the late Eighteenth Century, Wesley, who was in love with her, asked her to marry him.)

MAN:

Be sweet and sympathetic of spirit. The mild tempered among you shall be exalted. Bring peace to the souls of men…

GRACE:

It was, first of all, our deep and abiding commitment to accomplishing the work of God that brought John and I together. As we came to know each other through the Society meetings, I grew to admire John for his forthright manner of speaking and his prudent consideration for women's work within religion. It pleased me to no end when one day, when we had been discussing the topic of women preaching in the pulpit, he said, "Since God has gifted many women with the ability to deliver pure, precise, and moral speech, who are we to question His eternal wisdom? It would appear He has no preference if male or female impart His scriptural advice."

On more than one occasion, John spoke in this manner and, over a brief time, endeared himself easily to me. So...

(Takes ring in case from box and opens case.)

when he asked me to marry him, well, I said I would. But…
it was not that I did not care deeply for John. I did. I durst not have become engaged to him, if I had not wished to be his wife. Truly there was nothing that could have made me feel so glad as to be married to John. But still, I was a widow and was used to having a husband who had stayed always with me near home and hearth...and had done my bidding. So I could only imagine the dismay I would feel toward John while he went about his itinerancy.

Lest you surmise that my actions were not sincere, let me assure you it was not lack of love that caused the break; it was an abundance of love. It was for his sake. Well, admittedly, mine too that I called off the marriage. Neither of us would have been happy. If I had kept John from his ministry, what would I have been to him but a millstone around his neck…and he to mine?

(Snaps ring case closed.)

Instead, I gladly accepted the leadership of the Visitors to the Sick. In this position, I could ease the suffering of the weak and ailing and not…well…not be so vexed.

(Places ring in case on altar.)

Rose Duchesne (1769~1852)

(Rose Philippine Duchesne's lifelong dream was to work with the Native American Indians.)

MAN:

Be content with what you have been given by the greater powers that rule this earth. Avoid the temptation to lust after that which you do not have...

ROSE:

I loved the stories Mother read to me, stories of the saints and martyrs. When I heard the words, I could picture them in my mind's eye and, more than anything, I wanted to be like them—virtuous. So, when I was ten, I started giving all I could to the poor, my little allowance, not very much, but all I had. When I was twelve, I became enchanted with the stories told by the Jesuit missionaries who visited our home.

(Removes Dream Catcher from box.)

I learned about the Indians of America and I wanted to help, to do the work of God, teach the unenlightened, tend the sick. I prayed that one day I would be able to do mission work in the foreign fields of America.

When I told my parents I wanted to enter a convent, they were frantic. Mother was beside herself...Father very angry, but not nearly as angry as, when, at seventeen, I refused to become betrothed to the young man he had chosen. When I entered the novitiate, my parents did not even attend the ceremony. I loved my parents very much. I did not want to cause them grief. But I knew I had been called by a higher power to care for and teach those of less good fortune than myself.

I joined the Ladies of Faith, a small society of women dedicated to the furthering of education for the young women of France. We developed three new convents and Sacred Heart schools. And I knew that we were ready to reach out, send missionaries to foreign lands such as America.

In 1819, Bishop William DuBourg in Louisiana, America, put out the call for religious women to come and open a school in his district. I was fifty years old when I crossed the ocean to answer his call. During the next several years, I assisted in the establishment of a school for girls, an orphanage, and the first Sacred Heart convent in America. And I prayed, still yearning to journey west to work with the Indians.

Permission was finally given to take the Word of God to the Potawatomi Indians. I had waited nearly all my life for this decision to be made. I was seventy-two that summer. And, as we traveled west to Sugar Creek, Kansas, the wonder of my youth passed before my eyes, and I knew I had finally come to the place in life where it no longer mattered what age I was. It only mattered that I was there.

(Places Dream Catcher on altar.)

Marie Laveau (1794~1881)

(Marie Laveau practiced both Voodoo and Catholicism in early Nineteenth Century New Orleans. She used her knowledge of sorcery and Black Magic to both obtain personal power and to help the poor and the sick.)

MAN:

Be humble of spirit. Cast your eyes downward and do not mock the men who keep you safe from harm. Banish your bold and brazen ways...

MARIE:

Many people, both the rich and the poor, came to me for help. Love potions, predicting the future, casting spells, curses—I was very good with these. They called me the Voodoo Queen, but they said it with respect. They feared me, you know. Powerful men came for help. Why should I not be powerful too? They paid me well. And why not? I could do for them what no one else could. Why should I not have a house as good as theirs?

I had guests who were used to having the best. Perhaps you know of them? General Jean Humbert? He fought the Battle of New Orleans. A decent man. I was the only woman of color to be invited to his funeral. And Jean Lafitte. He served with General Andrew Jackson. They fought the British at New Orleans. And who could forget the Marquis de Lafayette, the great Revolutionary War hero? All close friends, who frequently visited New Orleans. Should I not have had a fine and comfortable place for them to converse, to celebrate, to lay their heads?

Yet, even though I was a woman of good business sense, I never turned my back on the poor. When they came to me, it was to ask for help for the hungry, the sick, the dying. I did what I could. I baked bread for the hungry. I washed the sick and dying. I dressed the dead and prepared them for burial. I asked nothing in return. They were my true and trusted friends.

As for the poor devils in prison, the convicts, I often fixed a special treat—gumbo—the likes of which they'd never eaten before. They dreamed about my sweet and delicious savory stew and begged me to cook it again and again, which I gladly did. And on the day before a hanging, I cooked the gumbo with particular care and added...

(Slips vial of poison out of bodice.)

just a pinch of...of magic. Imagine the astonishment of the jailers when they came to get the prisoner and found he had already expired.

(Places vial of poison on altar.)

Gladys Aylward (1904~1970)

(When the China Inland Mission Center of London turned Gladys Aylward down for missionary work in China, she saved the money she earned as a parlor maid until she had enough for her passage. In 1930, she arrived in a small mountain town, Shansi, just south of Peking (Beijing) eager to spread the word of the Christian Bible.)

MAN:

Do not forever desire to move beyond the station of your calling. Avoid the seeds of ambition. These sins are not easily forgiven...

GLADYS:

Nothing could dampen the exhilarating feeling of joy I experienced as I boarded the train in London. Not even the inevitable difficulties of travel—the screeching of the train along the rails to Vladivostok; the dizzying pitch and tilt of the ship to Japan; the stench of the overcrowded trains and buses to Peking; the precarious ride over rocky ledge on the back of a mule—for I was finally realizing my dream, to spread the Word of God in China.

Becoming a foot-inspector, however, was not what I had envisioned as part of my spiritual mission. In London, I had encountered hunger, disease, and violence. I had seen women begging in the streets, children thin and pale clutching their mothers' skirts. But I had never seen anything—not anything as appalling as the suffering of the women of China. Not the poor women who worked in the rice paddies. No, not the poor women...rather the women of position, the upper class who had been so harmed. So severe were their deformities that many could not walk at all. And those who could, tottered along barely able to move from one room to another.

(Retrieves shoes from box.)

Not for a minute had I ever dreamed I would be asked to work with the Chinese government to enforce the decree to end the practice of foot binding female children. The Mandarin himself came to me with this request. I could not say, "No."

It was this remarkable event—a miracle, really—which allowed me contact with the Chinese women within their private realms. Where we came to know each other and our individual ways. And where they became my captive audience and I was given the perfect opportunity to convert them to my Christian faith.

(Places shoes on altar.)

Kateri Tekakwitha (1656~1680)

(Kateri Tekakwitha defied her Mohawk tribe by refusing to marry and instead choosing to embark on a life of virginal devotion to the Christian God. Disfigured and almost blinded by smallpox, Kateri became known as the "Lily of the Mohawks" when, immediately upon her demise, all traces of her deformities vanished.)

MAN:

Like the gracious pure and lovely lily, a woman must be virginal in thought, word, and deed. Let her scourge and pierce, if she finds herself lacking…

KATERI:

Tekakwitha, one who fixes things. This was the name given me by my parents, my father, a Mohawk tribal chief of the Iroquois, and my mother, a Christian Algonquin, captured by the Iroquois and saved from slavery by my father. In my fourth year, a great plague came to our village. It swept through, taking with it both my parents. Some say it was a miracle I survived.

Pitted by the pox, I was left weak of body, but never weak of spirit. When the missionaries came, I learned of the Christian God. I remembered my mother having told me about Him. And I knew I wanted to serve Him…only Him…with my life. And nothing could change my mind. When I refused to marry, my tribal relatives of the Turtle Clan demoted me from daughter of the stars to slave of the earth. They were greatly angered, when this did not change my way of thinking.

I was forced to flee for my life. In Canada, I found refuge in the cabin of Anastasia Tegonhatsihonga, a good Christian woman. Devoted to living our lives in prayer, purity, and provision of the poor and sick, Anastasia and I petitioned the Jesuits to let us start our own sisterhood. But they refused. They said no Indian woman had ever entered a convent.

(Retrieves icon from box and shows it to audience.)

Kateri, *Catherine,* this was the name given me by the Jesuits. They named me after the Catholic saint, Catherine of Sienna, a woman who had lived her life in prayer and penance and healed the wounded, sick, and dying. They named me after Catherine, but would not allow me, a Mohawk, to participate fully in the sisterhood of God.

(Places icon on altar.)

Frances Willard (1839~1898)

(An 1880's educator and suffragist, Frances Willard's concern for the social status of women led her to activism for the Women's Christian Temperance Union. She believed that women could achieve political authority through the Temperance Movement.)

MAN:

Meddling women disrupt the workings of society and make the world a dangerous place for others. A worthy heart is a peaceful heart...

FRANCES:

(Removes liquor bottle from box.)

I have just a few remarks to make this evening. I want to talk to you, just briefly, about two things, idleness and intemperance. In my day, women fought for the right to vote. And won. But today, there are other significant issues, which must be addressed. For example, the seduction of the female gender through lewd and licentious photographic pictures; the beatings of wives and children in their homes by inebriated husbands; the suppression of women's freedom to choose that which will not harm their own bodies, just to name a few. Women, if you are to obtain political power, change the face of the future, you must not sit idly by and accept the dictates of a society drunk with male superiority.

And, having said that, I would like to continue by cautioning you all, women and men, against immoderation. The attainment of high spirits should not be gained through an overindulgence of distilled spirits. Imbibing in hard liquor, any liquor at all for that matter, is injurious to both the physical and mental aspects of the good health given you by our gracious Lord. Alcoholism is an affliction of the weak. It is without a doubt an invitation to slovenliness, deceit, and violence.

The Women's Christian Temperance Union has been these many years doing its best to nurture the public by raising awareness of the problem with *Drink—Drink,* the devil's device—for rupturing the roots of the human family. Neither family, nor individual, can survive the *Drink*. A drunkard in the house is like a snake in the grass and must be prohibited from slithering forth.

God willing, you will take heed of this insidious state of affairs, join your energies to the Union, and fulfill your obligations to your fellow citizens.

(Places liquor bottle on altar.)

Regina Jonas (1902~1944)

(Regina Jonas, born in Berlin, Germany in 1902, graduated from the Academy for the Science of Judaism as a teacher of religion, and was the first woman to be ordained a rabbi.)

MAN:

The pulpit is no place for a woman. She should instead speak softly in quiet soothing tones, remembering always that the voice of patience, kindness, and duty carries with it a powerful certainty that all is well with the world…

REGINA:

(Removes Jewish Star on chain from box and slips it on.)

I had great difficulty becoming ordained. No woman had ever served in this capacity and there was concern—great concern—that having a woman as a rabbi would cause problems, serious problems with the Jewish Orthodox rabbinate. However, after several disappointments and refusals, I was finally ordained in 1935 by Rabbi Max Dienemann in Offenbach.

As a teacher of religion, I had worked in both public and private schools with no difficulty in finding a position. However, as a rabbi, I could not locate a single synagogue that would accept a female preacher. I had to take whatever I could. I worked for a time as a chaplain for Jewish social organizations, and then…

And then the war came and my expertise was needed. So many of the rabbis had either left Germany or had been ordered into forced labor that even a woman rabbi became acceptable. As incomprehensible as this may seem, it is what happened and what allowed me to preach in the pulpits of the synagogues.

But the sense of victory was fleeting. I had barely begun my new work when I was ordered to list all my property. Two days later, I was arrested by the Gestapo and deported to the camp at Theresienstadt where I was interned from 1942 until 1944.

I did what I could to help the others cope, knowing full well that my messages of assurance were, in all truth, empty of hope. Still, I was one of the fortunate few who had a mission to consume my mind. Comforting others was a true gift from God. It produced for me a kind of peaceful relief, which sustained and spurred me ever onward, until, in 1944, I was deported to Auschwitz...

(Slips off Jewish Star and places it on altar.)

Eliza Snow (1804~1887)

(In the early 1800's, Eliza Snow's family left their Baptist faith to join the Mormon community in Nauvoo, Illinois.)

MAN:

A woman without a man is like a rudderless vessel, adrift on a raging sea. Bend to the task of womanhood and dedicate your service to God and man. Wear your dedication like a banner for all to see...

ELIZA:

Shards of fractured amber light flicker and fall like breaking splintering glass over purple morning mountains, mountains rising ever upward to the heavens above. And one can see that God rests not. Nor do I, as thoughts emerge, poignant and pure, then evolve into shattered parables, tinged with the color of pain. The events, the faces—unmarred by age—remain as clear today as they once were so long ago and I am remembering...remembering...

(Removes bouquet of flowers from box.)

I was sealed to the Prophet Joseph Smith, the only man I ever loved, for life, in 1842. Nor did I know our time together would be so shortened that I would be, only two years later moving west, a widow, with the Saints. We had come to Nauvoo to find peace. But, in exile, we departed.

Those who tormented us, the angry mob who stormed the Carthage jail and shot my husband and his comrades were of a mind that plural marriage was nothing less than whoredom. Now, that was the farthest thing from truth one could ever imagine. It was our God-given responsibility to provide new souls for His glory and praise. How better to accomplish this reverent task?

We were given two weeks to plan and pack our wagons for the trip west. Armed guards were placed about our community to protect us from Mormon oppressors. But it was often the guards themselves who haunted us, their icy stares silently mocking.

When we settled in the new country, I became wife to the Prophet Brigham Young and joined my sister wives. As a woman, wife, and President of the Relief Society, I was always treated fairly and with great respect. In Carthage, my life had been threatened if I took up pen and ink and told the true tale of the killings there. But in my new home I found my private place among my brothers and sisters as a poet whose work was met with grateful praise. And, though it is tormenting to admit, had God not sent to me such perfect pain, I could not have set it into verse.

As the sun slips silently over purple mountain peaks and departs the day, my heart cries out, 'Jehovah, be praised' and I place my cares aside and rest, setting memories free, scattering them like wild flowers on the winds of time.

(Places flowers on altar.)

Ann Lee (1736~1784)

(Born in Manchester, England to a working class family, Ann Lee married at a young age and gave birth to four children. All four were either stillborn or died shortly after birth. Through a vision, she came to believe that she was the female Christ and, from this revelation, went on to form the Shaker religion.)

MAN:

One should not have to be reminded that woman was formed from Man's rib, that she led her husband into a sinful existence, and that she gained the loss of paradise for them both. One should not have to be reminded...

ANN:

(Removes wooden cross from box.)

Married I was and still working in the cotton factory, when I got to know the Wardley's, James and Jane. Jane had gotten the calling and James, too, and they had left the Society of Friends to go and preach the new testimony of the truth. The second coming was to be soon, they said. It could be man or woman. No one knew upon whom God would lay His hand.

He came to me in the dark of night and laid His hand upon my shoulder. "Ann," He said, "you have been chosen to take up my ministry." His face was kind but rugged and determined as He held my hand in His and demanded my answer. And from the wilderness of my soul, came a voice crying out, "Yes, yes, yes. I will lead your people to the new land. And there we will build a community, a congregation dedicated to the mission of God."

I had heard that those seeking safety from the tyranny of the Anglican Church of England had found freedom in the colonies, so I gathered the few together and we journeyed 'cross the sea. But, once there, our United Society of Believers was sorely accepted.

(Holds up the cross.)

"Take up your cross. Leave the carnal ways of the devil behind. Turn your hands to work and hearts to God," I pleaded. But many outside our group of Believers were offended that a woman had the insolence to speak in such a way. For my wish to lead others to perfection—perfection in God's eyes—I was suspected of witchcraft. I was stoned, thrown in prison, and beaten by mobs of good religious people—people who could not comprehend that God had, this time, chosen a female Christ.

(Places wooden cross on altar.)

Mary Dyer (1611~1660)

(Mary Dyer gave her life on the gallows to free her fellow Quakers from religious persecution. After her death, Charles II, King of England forbid all further killings of Quakers in Boston.)

MAN:

Holy women do not break the barriers of religious worship. They comply with given standards and bow to conformity. Like the weeping willow, they bend to the winds of men's wisdom and writs…

MARY:

Tyrannized as we were by the Church of England, my husband William and I sailed with our children to John Winthrop's Massachusetts Bay Colony, where we sought freedom to worship as we chose. But what we found, instead, was worse injustice at the hands of narrow-minded men. No one, it turned out, was allowed beliefs that differed from the Puritan way.

When I met Anne Hutchinson, my life turned for the better. She was of a mind that women should be heard and what she had to say was gratifying. She did not believe in the Covenant of Works, that people could get to heaven by doing good and following the rules. What she believed in made much more sense—The Covenant of Grace—that people could never do enough good works to be worthy enough of God, but that God was generous and would welcome home those who had complete faith. After Anne was arrested for holding meetings in her home to discuss Sunday sermons and her views, she was banned from the community. But we remained true and devoted friends. And I was devastated, when Anne—forced to move to the wilderness with her children—was massacred by the Pequot Indians.

Seeking new life, I returned for a time to England where I met George Fox, who led us in worship, who told me over and over that women are equal to men, that we must venture forth to spread the Seeds of the Seekers. I sailed back to my husband and children…a Quaker, but, even as my ship docked, I was taken into custody and thrown into prison. No Quakers were allowed to practice their beliefs.

(Retrieves rope from box.)

I was reprieved the first time from hanging by my husband's letter of petition to Governor Endicott and the General Court. But I knew I must make a plea for freedom of worship. And though I could have turned against my beliefs and away from the rope, I did not. I went to the gallows with the knowledge that I...a woman...would not be giving up my life in vain.

(Places rope on altar.)

Elizabeth Seton (1774~1821)

(Elizabeth Ann Seton founded the Sisters of Charity and Roman Catholic parochial education in the United States.)

MAN:

A woman shall cleave to her husband and follow his guidance for he will protect her and provide for her a safe haven from harm. She shall have no worry, nor care, nor fear, if she places her trust in him...

ELIZABETH:

When William died unexpectedly, I was left with five children to support and no source of income. While William was alive, his business had prospered. But when he became ill, everything changed. We had traveled to Italy in hopes of improving his health with a warmer climate. But, once there, his health rapidly dwindled. And there I was in a foreign country, alone and frightened with the prospect of beginning a new life.

With the urging of William's relatives, I found comfort in the compassionate care of their Roman Catholic faith. And, in my conversion, I discovered newfound hope.

(Retrieves crucifix from box)

By the time I returned to America, I felt relieved to be going home and renewed of spirit. But that renewal was to last only a short time for, upon my return, I learned that my family had disinherited me for leaving their Episcopal Church.

I was now more alone than ever and I knew I must do something quickly to aid my children and myself. But what? What could I do? Become a domestic helper? Nurse? Teach? Yes, I would teach. I would start a school, a school for young women. And this is exactly what I did. And, in doing so, I was able to feed, clothe, and care for my children so that they could grow strong of body, mind, and soul.

No matter the extent of difficulties that life brings, a woman can always depend on her own God-given strength, intelligence, and power to make the choices necessary for positive change. Soon after establishing the school for girls, I founded The Sisters of Charity, a new order of women who would teach, nurse, and help the poor. But even as life became pleasant and good, I often reminded myself of the early days, the days of insecurity and fear and how I had come to realize that faith in my own abilities was the real answer to all my prayers.

(Places crucifix on altar.)

Aimee Semple McPherson (1890~1944)

(Aimee Semple McPherson, evangelist and faith healer, was a woman of great determination who, with her mother, built a 5,000-seat temple in which to do her personal preaching.)

MAN:

Women must not display themselves as spectacles for all to see. They must retain the dignity and warmth they were given at birth. May the angels sing hymns of praise for those who shield themselves in stillness and in solitude...

AIMEE:

(Retrieves bell from box and rings it at intervals throughout.)

Good evening and welcome everyone! I am Sister Aimee Semple McPherson and I cherish this opportunity to share even a few brief moments with you. Some say, I'm Pentecostal. Some say, Baptist. It makes no difference to me. I am here to lead you all—yes, all—to our heavenly host above.

I am known for my evangelism, finding the lost sheep and bringing them back to the fold and for being the first woman to use the airwaves to preach a radio gospel program. I am also recognized as the first female to drive across the United States without a man. What do they think we women are? Helpless? Ha! Ha! When Minnie, my mother, and I set our minds to something, nothing stood in our way. We packed up the two children, painted the words, GOSPEL CAR, on our 1918 Oldsmobile, and set off for California with nary a worry nor a care. For we had faith, faith that God would see us through. And, of course, He did, just as He will do for you.

As a faith healer, I amazed everyone, including myself! All those sweet suffering little children, rising up from their wheelchairs, tossing their crutches aside, reaching out to embrace the spirit of His divine love...the reporters questioned how those miracles occurred. Why, it was faith!

Simple faith, people! When our loving Savior saw their trust and faith, His spirit descended upon them in no time at all to comfort and console.

And it was faith that filled my 5000-seat Angeles Temple to overflowing each and every night. Why everyone flocked there to hear me preach the sermon of the day. Those were the brilliant days of glory and praise. Now, let me just ask you to pray with me: Praise the Lord! Praise His people! Praise the women! Praise them all! Praise God for blessing them with the courage and daring to renew the earth!

(Places bell on altar. Retrieves Fanny Crosby's dark glasses from box, then goes to Fanny and leads her to center stage. Sits while Fanny recites her speech. Then guides her to altar and finally back to her chair.)

Fanny Crosby (1820~1915)

(Accidentally blinded by an unlicensed country doctor, who incorrectly applied hot mustard poultices to her eyes at the age of six weeks, Fanny Crosby went on to write over five thousand inspirational hymns of Christian praise.)

MAN:

A woman is free to make her own choices, but she must not transgress the limits of the law. Sanctified women are enshrined in a golden glaze of glory. But those filled with guile and guilt shall be cast into darkness...

FANNY:

(Accepts dark glasses from Aimee McPherson. Reads speech with fingertips as if it is written in Braille.)

Many wondered why I was not enraged with the country doctor who caused me to become sightless. "He blinded you! Why do you forgive him as you do?" they would ask. Forgive? There was nothing to forgive, for I feel certain that the accidental blinding of my eyes as an infant was part of a larger design, which no human hand could have contrived. The loss of outer sight gave me a depth of inner sight that could only be considered a great and wonderful blessing.

And what is blindness anyway? Who are the blind? It was not I, who was blind. It was the many who could not, or would not, see the miracles of His light. And I was deeply troubled by this, the blind ways of sinners. Somehow I knew I must do my part to lead them to the gift of clear and conscious vision. I prayed for answers.

The prayers in my heart took flight, winging their way through words patterned into poetry, forming the melodies of faith and love. I take no credit for this heavenly talent, knowing for certain it was His guiding hand, which led me to create a clear and cloudless vision for His people through Christian song. My mind poured forth the words to over five thousand hymns. There were so many that I used more than one hundred thirty pseudonyms. It was not a necessity that my name be credited for all to know the countless litanies I had created. It was only important that the multitudes shared in the sweet symphony of His embrace, and opened their eyes and hearts to the precious mysteries and wonders of His love.

(Guided by Aimee to altar, she places glasses upon it and is then led back to her chair.)

Helena Petrovna Blavatsky (1831~1891)

(Helena Petrovna Blavatsky was the founder of the Theosophical Society, a worldwide association dedicated to the belief that there is one divine spirit to which all people are universally connected.)

MAN:

Woman, temptress of the virtuous man, do not contaminate and corrupt him with your seductive ways. Do not lure him into sin. Hide your beguiling bodies beneath the scarf and habit. Torture him not with your evil acts…

HELENA:

(Plucks crown of stars from box and sets it on her head.)

I am Madame Helena Petrovna Blavatsky, spiritualist, founder of the Theosophical Society, and telepathic maharini of the truth. And I am tired of hearing the rubbish and lies about women circulated through the centuries by religious communities. Enough, I say! From the beginning of time, women have been called evil and blamed for the blasphemous behavior of men. It is not enough that women are told they must be servile, submissive, and secondary to men, but they are also told they must silently accept this unfair and humiliating status. This must stop!

As a mystic, spiritualist, and naturalist, I have traveled the world over, studying and writing of the wisdom of the One Divine Spirit and our connection to each other through the Spirit. And, I will tell you that the Spirit does not wish for women to be cast into roles of degradation and despair. In my travels, I have met brave and daring women; women such as those you have met this evening—visionaries, victors, victims…

HELENA:

*(**WOMAN 1 & 2** stand.)*

martyrs, missionaries, mystics…

HELENA:

*(**WOMAN 3** stands.)*

many of whom defied the rules of religious men…

HELENA:

*(***WOMAN 4 & 5** *stand.)*

others who fell prey to their violence and shed the blood of saints. All of whom had the courage to defy the dictates of a society saturated with irrationality and inequity!

I entreat you all to remember the stories, the substance and the spirit of these women who have challenged the tempests of time to appear before you this very night to break the silence and unveil the secrets of their souls. They are—as brilliant stars among the planets shining in perpetual hope—an example for us all to follow.

(Places crown on altar.)

WOMAN 1

(Turns and moves forward.)

For too long women have suffered under a stifling shroud of silence...

WOMAN 2

(Turns and moves forward. Stands opposite **WOMAN 1.***)*

In the name of religion...we have been cast into the shadows...

WOMAN 3

(Turns to audience.)

Relegated to roles of submission and servitude...ordered to be obedient...

MAN

It is your place to be obedient!

WOMEN 1 ~ 6

(In unison, all turn to face **MAN**, *forcing him to sit.)*

No! We do not have to accept that kind of thinking any longer.

(All turn, in unison, to audience.)

We can band together to stop the injustice!

WOMAN 4

Doubt not yourselves, nor your sisters, for it is time to put an end to enslavement.

WOMAN 5

Remove your masks of misery. Rise up and rebel against injustice!

WOMAN 6

Take charge of your future!

WOMEN in UNISON

(All come forward and stand together at center stage.)

We give you our lives and these sacrificial offerings as symbols of wisdom, courage, and hope.

MAN

(He sits, defeated by the women and their strength of purpose.)

WOMEN in UNISON

(To the strains of Fanny Crosby's hymn, Blessed Assurance, the women leave the stage, their mission complete.)

The End

Properties

BISHOP, BRIDGET	Paring Knife
BOSANQUET-FLETCHER, MARY	Methodist materials
LUTHER, KATHARINA	Rosary
BROWN, OLYMPIA	Prayer book & ballot
WESLEY, SUSANNA	Bible
BESANT, ANNIE	Book
HOSOKAWA, GRACIA	Icon
JUDSON, ANN HASSELTINE	Framed wedding photo
CLITHEROW, MARGARET	Medieval crucifix
WILKINSON, JEMIMA	Stone
MURRAY, GRACE	Engagement ring
DUCHESNE, ROSE PHILIPPINE	Dream catcher
LAVEAU, MARIE	Vial of poison
AYLWARD, GLADYS	Small shoes
TEKAKWITHA, KATERI	Icon
WILLARD, FRANCES	Liquor bottle
JONAS, REGINA	Jewish star
SNOW, ELIZA	Wild flowers
LEE, ANN	Cross
DYER, MARY BARRETT	Rope
SETON, ELIZABETH	Crucifix
McPHERSON, AIMEE SEMPLE	Bell
CROSBY, FRANCES JANE	Dark glasses
BLAVATSKY, HELENA	Crown of stars

Reflections on Women and Religion

Coralie Cederna Johnson

Spiritual Heritage of the Lakotas

Wawokiya Win, *Helpful Woman,* in her essay *Our Grandfather The Great Spirit*, speaks of the rich spiritual heritage of her people, the Lakotas—named *Sioux* (*cutthroat* or *snake in the grass*) by the French. Win explains that, although these white men came to her country, persecuted the Lakota, and created destruction, her people held fast to their religious beliefs. These beliefs included respect for all things natural, honor of God as Great Spirit and Grandfather, and love of Grandmother Earth, female creation of God, who as mother and nurturer of all children provides food for the body, mind, and soul in a *Circle of Life*.

The Lakota's respect for God, each other, and all things natural..."the trees, rocks, flowers, the four-legged, two-legged, all things that crawl and the winged ones"...is particularly pleasing to me who loves all of nature. I, too, as the Lakota, find God in every natural thing and see "the breath of life given to each race and species as a wondrous part of the Great Spirit." I find a deep sense of God's presence within the natural wonders of our world. Orange-red squirrel, blue-green sea, red-violet sunset—these simple miracles are, for me, some of the most important connections to spirituality for I find in them the peace that I believe the Great Spirit wishes us to know and enjoy within our days on earth.

The Lakota sense of community and caring for each other, including those less fortunate within the band or camp, is to be admired. This, along with the importance of family and giving praise to each other, brings emphasis to their belief that members of their tribe are of one mind and one spirit.

Along the "path of beauty and enlightenment," honor is not reserved for keeping holy only one special day a week, but is expressed freely each and every day from dawn to dusk. If I could rewrite Christianity's Ten Commandments, I would change, "Remember, keep holy the Sabbath Day," to "Remember, keep holy (and rejoice) in each new day the Lord, the Great Spirit, provides."

Win's people, who call themselves *Ikci-wicasa*, meaning *common people* or *natural people,* honor the natural laws of honesty, courage, fortitude, generosity, piety, respect, and humbleness. I am especially moved by a religion in which there is no sin. And where there is love and respect for God and for all others, but which wisely lacks in man-made religious/political laws. And where purity of hearts along life journeys proclaims peace. With respect to Win and her Lakota people, I wish to call myself *Ikci-wicasa*.

Taoism: Path of Harmony

In *Voice of God, Mother of Life,* Zhang I. Hsien explains that Taoism is simple yet mysterious. Tao is a path of harmony. It is nature. It is the voice of God. It is a philosophy of creating excellence in life with eventual immortality. Tao is good and evil, day and night, light and dark, women and men. But, for Hsien, Tao is the "mother of life."

Hsien, whom I prefer to refer to as Lily, because of her deep love for nature's beauty, seems like a lovely modern-day flower of life as she works on learning more each day about the ancient Chinese philosophy of Taoism. Having left her home at the age of six to study with Taoist Master E.F. Chang for the next twenty-seven years, she has become a healer of the body, mind, and heart.

Devoted doctor, psychic, and priest, she is also a poet and describes Tao as mother of life in lilting verse:

> *Mother of life wakes her children early in the morning*
> *by lifting her silken curtain to suggest the beginning of a*
> *new day. With a gentle kiss, she wakes up the trees, leaves*
> *and branches, streams, rivers and seas and orchestrates*
> *the symphony of nature.*

Reading Lily's stunning words, I am drawn into her passion for Taoism as mother of life.

As with the Lakota's *Mother Earth* in Wawokiya Win's essay, Tao's *Mother of Life* provides for all, giving food for body, mind, and spirit.

With Heaven, the *Father,* she has conceived and given birth to son *Water* who always seeks his lowest level in order to find balance; daughter *Lake* who fills in the holes for *Water* and helps balance things with life-giving water energy; son *Thunder* whose loud voice guides the others with important announcements; daughter *Wind* who carries pollen on her wings for procreation and blows a cool refreshing breeze; daughter *Fire* who, through metamorphosis, allows "old" life to ebb away in order to make new life possible; and son *Mountain* who is strength and silence.

Lily, who tells us she has had many lives, observes that some people, seeking happiness and wealth, fail to appreciate the simple things in life.

"It seems that with just a little effort or with no effort at all you can attain Tao and feel free," she says.

And it is clear that Lily's love of Tao has brought her the great joy of feeling free and alive..."We can experience Tao in many simple ways—the rushing of a river, wind blowing through the trees, the heady fragrance of flowers, birds singing, fish jumping...while dancing with Tao, my breath, my arms and legs are moving and meditating with the superior spirit, I am part of the universal movement and I feel so alive!" And I feel free and alive simply sharing her thoughts.

Witchcraft Honors Life Cycles

"I am a woman seeking to know, love, and trust female wisdom and strength within me and others. I need a female image of divinity to connect with the deep waters of my own spirit." So speaks Antiga in her essay, *The Goddess in Me,* of her search for soul and discovery of the Goddess within which led her into the practice of a feminist spirituality called witchcraft.

Witchcraft, Antiga explains, is a pre-Christian religion, which "honors earth cycles and images divinity in a female form—the Goddess who brings the world to life." Rather than trying to exert power over or control the world's creatures, witchcraft honors the flowing of life cycles and values each creature for its contributions. The guidelines under which witches live are two:

- Do no harm to others, including one's self.
- Whatever energy one puts into the world returns three-fold.

Antiga practices Dianic witchcraft, which is based on the philosophical principles of Feminism, a set of beliefs that recognizes the often overlooked female contributions to society and which:

- Values female perspective as an essential part of the human experience
- Affirms and empowers women

- Encourages women to define themselves, know they can have and create choices, and can trust themselves...and...
- Teaches women to love, respect, and trust other women exactly as they are.

The beliefs of feminism, along with spirituality, "the experience of connecting with the divine," have led Antiga and other women to find, within witchcraft, the Goddess within. "What I expect my spirituality to give me is an ever-increasing ability to get my ego out of the way and let Goddess energy flow through," says Antiga.

Unlike male-based and biased religions, witchcraft nurtures, empowers, and respects women. It does not seek the patriarchal pyramid, which places only a select few near the top, with women at its base. Instead it encourages equality through a circle-based structure that helps and encourages women to seek balance in their inner and outer worlds, seek out and connect with other women, and become more aware of how their actions affect others.

Antiga explains that her experience of the Goddess is both "internal and external." Internally, she feels the energy of the Goddess emanate from the earth, the trees, a rainbow, and the warmth of friends. She does not describe her own external images of the Goddess, but states that these images can be whatever, and as many, as anyone wishes them to be. And though her images of the Goddess may be different from someone else's, there is no "one right way of envisioning and approaching the Goddess." The important thing is that they are meaningful and useful to each individual.

For Antiga, the discovery of the Goddess has brought her to a female-centered spirituality within which she practices witchcraft with other women by following ancient traditions. In covens, small groups of thirteen or fewer members, honor and perform rituals in celebration of the cycles of the moon, the turning of the seasons, and the return of light and dark each year, conjoining the members to the earth, the earth's creatures and plants, and each other. The connection of the 28-day lunar cycle and women's menstrual cycles is honored as in ancient times. Other life-enriching rituals have been created to help release despair and encourage empowerment.

The Triple Goddess, a trinity that predates patriarchal religions, consists of Maiden, Mother, and Crone, each depicting a reverent aspect of women:

> The Maiden conveys an image of independence and self-sufficiency. She is the child, the sexually free young woman, and reminds that the lives of all children are sacred.
>
> The Mother represents creativity and procreativity. She creates, nurtures, and accomplishes.
>
> The Crone exemplifies the older woman, who has gained wisdom and strength to share, who is teacher and counselor, and who is a model for accepting life as it is.

It was through the discovery of the Triple Goddess that Antiga realized the pain caused by a lack of the Divine Female in her upbringing. She then began to find the female divinity in many places—nature, art and songs by feminists—but most importantly within herself. "Finding the Goddess brought me home to myself," she says. "Honoring the Goddess in my life encourages me to feel whole and valuable as a woman."

Antiga's essay was enlightening and interesting to me, for whom witchcraft previously had been only occasional, murky musings of people entertaining peculiar practices, ideas, and beliefs. From my perspective, any religion, spirituality, or set of beliefs and/or principles should be honored if it, as witchcraft does, encourages a circle-based equality, women encouraging other women to work toward freedom of thought, self-empowerment, and respect for all earth's creatures.

As each woman makes her individual search for spirituality, I feel strongly that it is wise to investigate a variety of avenues of connecting to God, both externally and internally; learn to feel the divine energy within; and then act out those ideals, giving freely of one's love in the form of respect, shared empowerment, encouragement, and trust. I believe, as do the Dianic witches, that it is through this sharing that we receive back our most important source of energy—a circular, spiritual energy that provides us with enduring strength to continue our own endless personal growth, which, in turn, helps promote the growth of others. For me, these are all gifts from God given freely to us so we may work, love, and create with kindness, care, and respect for self and others.

Yearning for Miracles

In her essay, *The Virgin of Polish Hill*, Carolyn Banks tells us the tale of Kotka, a young Polish Catholic girl and her Aunt Clara. It seems that Aunt Clara is the lucky one, always winning at bingo, raffles, and special drawings. Now she's seen the Virgin Mary, Mother of God. When the Polish Catholic fans of Mary wind through the streets, making their way to the hill on which sits the psychiatric ward, one wonders who the crazy people really are—the psychiatric patients in the hospital on the hill, or the neighborhood people led by boozy Aunt Clara?

There is nothing to see, observes Kotka.

Perhaps, we see what we want to see. For these friends and neighbors of Aunt Clara, their reality was that one of their own had finally been blessed with a vision. With their knowledge of reported visitations of the Virgin Mary in such humble places of the world as Guadalupe, Lourdes, and Fatima—and their pilgrimages through the streets honoring these events—they were ready to believe. These devoted Catholic people were certain that one day the Virgin Mary would come to honor them, the Polish people, as well.

They knew the stories well. In Guadalupe, Mexico, 1531, Mary appeared, surrounded by bird song and bright light, to Juan Diego, an Indian of little education. The lady's garment, they had heard, was a cloak complete with an artistic rendering of the Virgin Mary, which brilliantly blended Catholicism and Indian culture, a visible sign of truth.

A peasant girl, Bernadette Soubirous of Lourdes, in the French Pyrenees, was host to the visits of Mary in 1858. A spring of water had erupted from the place of visitation and hundreds of thousands from around the world had endeavored to touch a drop of the precious liquid. The Roman Catholic Church had acknowledged the miracle as truth and young Bernadette was canonized a saint in 1933.

In a poor rural area of Portugal, 1917, the Virgin Mary once again appeared to the lowly and humble, Lucia, Francisco, and Jacinta, aged seven to ten years old. Once the secret was out, crowds thronged to the place of the miracles. It had been reported that on October 13, 1917, more than twenty thousand people awaited the virgin's coming, and although only the children saw the Virgin Mary, the crowds of many saw colored lights coupled with strange dancing movements in the sun.

Why should the Mexican people, the French, and the Portuguese have there own visitation by the Virgin Mary and not the Polish? Kotka's family and neighbors believed that it could certainly happen. So, when Aunt Clara, well known for her luck, reported her own special visitation, they were not only ready, but also eager to accept it as truth.

Only the child Kotka questioned what they were doing, why they believed her beer-swilling Aunt. She saw no virgin on the hill. She observed only the mind-boggling frenzy of a mob.

Kotka's story brings back many reminiscences of my growing up years in a small ethnic, mostly Roman Catholic, neighborhood, in a time when miracles were too scarce and people yearned for them to occur as they had in the stories of long ago saints.

My own *miraculous vision* occurred when I was eleven years old. We had just finished junior choir practice at Blessed Sacrament Catholic Parish, our newly built church, in Stambaugh, Michigan. Having prepared hymns for the following Sunday's mass, my friends had quickly disappeared into the icy winter night, heading for the warmth of their homes, leaving the choir director, Mrs. Marie Anderson, and me, the organist, to lock up the organ, put our black St. Basil's hymnals away, and tidy up before hiking down the mile-long hill toward home.

While Mrs. Anderson stood at the door waiting for me, I dipped my fingers into the holy water fountain, made the sign of the cross, and genuflected. Glancing into the windows of the church as I dipped, signed, and bent, I was astonished to see fractured lights in the perfect formation of stars dazzling the frosted glass.

"Mrs. Anderson," I whispered, "I see stars, in the windows."

She looked into every window in the church, but saw nothing except icy panes.

"Coralie," she gasped, "maybe you have seen a vision! You must tell your parents and the priest. Maybe you are a saint."

Now, mind you, I didn't think for a minute that this could be true. I may have only been eleven, but I knew better than that. However, I *had* seen the stars, and I had agreed to talk to my parents about it.

Though they were skeptical, my parents agreed that, since Mrs. Anderson had told me to, I should go and talk to the priest about the *vision*. Embarrassed and stammering, I did as my parents directed.

"Come with me," Father Freiburger said. We went to the windows, but there were no stars. "Now kneel down," he instructed, "and tell me what you see."

"Stars," I answered, relieved. At least I had not been imagining.

"Yes, stars," he smiled. "You have to look out at just the right angle, but there are definitely stars there. Those windows are the latest things on the market. We couldn't afford stained glass, so had to settle for these. So, there's your miracle. But don't worry. Maybe a real one will come your way, one of these days. We don't have a saint named Coralie. But that would be nice."

I was pretty sure I saw him wink as he disappeared up behind the altar.

The Goddesses of Hinduism

The goddesses of Hinduism have many faces and functions. There are goddesses associated with particular places in nature such as rivers; goddesses who preside over and protect villages from demons, disease, and enemies; and goddesses associated with wealth, power, and death. The earth itself is seen as the great goddess Prithivi. But, according to David Kinsley, author of *Sacred Female Imagery and Women's Religious Experience in Hinduism,* it seems there is no goddess to protect Hindu women from a long history of victimization by men.

From the majority of written sources in the Hindu tradition, it is clear that females have been made to be completely dependent on and subservient to males. The most famous Hindu Law Book, the *Law Book of Manu,* dictates that young women are to be held under the control of their fathers; married women under control of their husbands; and widows under the control of their sons. Women are thought to be dangerous and irresponsible without the control of men. Thus the woman's role in this society is to serve males, give birth to sons, and nourish men.

In Hindu writings, there are four stages of life for men:

- Student
- Householder
- Forest dweller and
- World renouncer.

However, females have only three very different stages of life:

- The unmarried young women, almost immediately after her first menstruation occurs, is expected to prepare for marriage by learning the art of pleasing a man and praying for sons to perpetuate her husband's lineage;

- Once married, the woman allies herself with her husband and his lineage and aspires to produce the sons she has prayed for;

- If her husband dies, the woman enters the third stage of life, that of widowhood. Hindu writing teaches her that she has lost the most important reason for living—even if she has sons—so she restricts herself to the simplest fare in foods, clothing without ornament, and often becomes a social outcast or recluse. Remarriage is rare and opposed.

In some parts of India, particularly Bengal and Rajasthan, the custom of *suttee* (widow suicide) is promoted, practiced, and praised. In death, a woman may finally come to be so honored for being a *good wife* that a shrine may even be built in her honor.

Suttee, as described in gory detail in Kinsley's article, explains that, as if departing on a joyous journey, the woman prostrates herself before the elders and asks for their blessings. With perfect tranquility, she climbs the ladder, sits down on the pyre, and tenderly takes her husband's head on her lap. Eve when the flames reach her, she maintains her composure and the crowd acclaims her as a good wife. (It is, in my opinion, one of the most appalling forms of female abuse in the world today. And I am chilled each time I think of these enslaved females whose minds have been indoctrinated to conclude that they have no rightful existence of their own.)

However, Kinsley tells us that anyone who spends a little time in India observing the everyday religious scene will see that women are supplied with rituals, festivals, and customs that are distinctively female-oriented and provide them with a satisfying and meaningful context in which to express their spirituality. Some women have assumed religious roles, some women have been famous saints, teachers, and gurus, and some practice special rituals called *vrats* (vows) which involve fasting and or abstention from certain types of foods, indulgences, or pleasures in order to obtain blessings or favors from a deity, usually for one of the males in the woman's immediate family.

Kinsley continues, "While a skeptic might argue that women's domestic rituals are often conducted especially for the welfare of the male members of the household, it seems clear that vrats and other rituals undertaken by women in the domestic sphere express and create a feeling of women's religious space in which they are in control of the most meaningful area of their lives."

It is not then surprising to me that some women have found an alternative to all this sordid business of marriage to a controlling Hindu human male by proclaiming a preference for the love of a Hindu God. Hindu literature produces many stories of women who have left their marriages to wander the hillsides, singing songs of passion and love for their *true* husbands. Such is the story of Mahadeviyakka who in the twelfth century C.E. went off to find the god Shiva, expressing to her deep longing to be entirely devoted to her *true* husband and her poems, sweet with passion.

Kinsley writes that women are actually "extremely active in almost every aspect of Hindu religion and in many areas dominate the scene." He concludes, "The male-oriented scriptures may prefer to understand women in supporting roles, as adjuncts to and nourishers of males. But in actual practice, women lead lives of their own that are religiously rich and distinctive."

Rich and distinctive? I am left reeling with the cruel and inhumane indignities these women have suffered at the hands of this male-based religion—a religion that brainwashes women into believing they live only to produce sons. A religion that, at the same time, tells them their female bodily fluids are regarded as so polluted that, during menstruation and following childbirth, they must be excluded from normal social contact and may not even be allowed to touch food for fear of befouling it for others.

The pollution, I say, is not in the women's bleeding, it is in the minds of those men who have created a foul existence for females from which there is, in most cases, no escape. The life these women are subjected to, in the name of religion, is horrendous. The idea of a living hell comes to mind, as I cannot imagine a place of worse misery.

Muslim Women in 20th Century Arab Thought

Since the beginning of this century, intellectual and political revolutionaries have tried to transform the Arab world with social change in order to "achieve parity" with the west, writes Yvonne Yazbeck Haddad in *Islam, Women, and Revolution in Twentieth-Century Arab Thought*. Western values advocated in educational institutions established by Christian missionaries were used as examples of superiority and "Islamic family law and regulations affecting the role and status of women were not only ridiculed as demeaning, but were also targeted as the cause of backwardness of Muslim societies." Three ideologies, the Nationalist, the Socialist, and the Islamist—"a scriptural form of religious piety offering the relevance of the Qur'an for everyday activity and insisting on regulation of all aspect of life"—have been the basis of discussion, argument, and debate.

While the nationalist's major concern was to free Arab people from foreign dominance and the socialist revolutionaries sought to bring economic development for the betterment of society, the Islamists' main focus was to make certain the principles of the Qur'an were followed, thereby preserving the family structure so as to save society from the hands of enemies.

All revolutionaries agreed that the condition of Muslim women was unacceptable and must be modified in order to preserve the whole of society. To all of the revolutionaries, Liberation of Women was seen as crucial, not so much for the individual but for the entire social system.

Qasim Amin, a lawyer who was one of the early advocates of women's liberation in the Arab world, argued for westernization and tried to show that the primary beneficiaries of this liberation of women would be men. He sought to have women uncover their faces, make their own marriage choices, and become educated so that they might be more knowledgeable mothers. However, religious leaders accused Amin of proposing changes that would denigrate women whose function, they believed, should be solely in the home, bearing children.

One of the major debates has been over education. While it was not entirely opposed for women, the content of education was debated. Traditional Muslims stated that, if changes were instituted in education for women, it would, "give pleasure to those foreigners...who seek to destroy Islam by changing its tenets." In all Islamist debates over women's liberation, the major concerns were:

- Whether or not a proposed change was consistent with, or deviated from, the Qur'an;
- Whether women could be respectable in public and not tempt lustful males and thereby undermine society and
- Whether changes would be in the best interest and goals of the Muslim society.

Considered the key to public morality, the modesty of women was viewed as most threatened by change: "...when the woman goes out naked into the street displaying her allurement to every seeker, arousing animal desire in the man, then there is no Islam, no religion, no doctrine."

Many changes have occurred since Qasim Amin's first efforts at awakening a reluctant society, but the contemporary vision of Muslim traditionalists and revolutionaries still perceives women's role as determined by her biological functions... "not only is she created to be pregnant, but more specifically all her roles are defined by her relations to the men in her life. She is rarely depicted as an independent person in her own right." A Saudi Arabian professor wrote, "[The woman] is a mother who nurtures her children forming men, a wife who beautifies life with her beloved smile, her tender touch soothing the ruggedness of the road and her expressive word easing the pressures of work..."

While work outside the home is still considered degrading by some Islamist traditionalists, many Muslim women today are lawyers, doctors, and engineers. There is a new generation of women who are not only, "educated in the liberal arts and sciences, but have also acquired Islamic literacy through study of the Qur'an." Along with their husbands, these women are helping build a better society. But many women, educated or not, see their most important role as supportive to society's needs by "reaching out from the sanctity of their homes to protect against moral degeneration and upholding the values that in the end will establish the "Kingdom of God" on earth."

I find it interesting that many Muslim women choose to veil their faces in public even though women of their grandmothers' era won the right to unveil. For this, they give many reasons such as:

- Religious: an act of obedience to the will of God; psychological, a return to Islamic roots and a rejection of western norms;
- Political: a sign of disenchantment with the prevailing political order;
- Cultural: a public affirmation of allegiance to chastity and modesty and...
- Domestic: a way to keep peace with the males in their respective families.

While some western philosophies interpret women's veiling and other signs of modesty and domesticity as inequality for Muslim women, it appears to me that the Islamic society of men and women have a common goal in which each and every person is equally concerned, and working toward, the betterment of their society.

Shaker Traditions

The Shakers, who gained their name because of their joyous quaking and shaking movements during religious services, were first founded in England by John and Jane Wardley, who believed and taught their flock that a second coming of Christ would probably appear to them in female form. That female form turned out to be Ann Lee, born in Manchester, England, 1736.

When Lee was twenty years old, she married Abraham Stanley and bore four children, all of who died either in childbirth or early childhood. Lee subsequently fell into a state of deep depression. She prayed constantly for release from her physical, spiritual, and emotional crisis.

When finally, several years later, she emerged from the depths of despair, she revealed to the Shaker community that she had witnessed a revelation from God that she was to be the second Christ.

She claimed God had also revealed to her that, at the root of all sin was lust, which led to all sexual relations. Based on this, she taught her followers that they should become celibate.

In 1774, Lee is reported to have had another revelation, this one to take her fold to America to spread the Gospel and "create God's kingdom on earth in the colonies." On the eve of the American Revolution, Lee and her people, who called themselves The United Society of Believers in Christ's Second Appearing, arrived in America, moved to upstate New York, and established the first Shaker communities in America.

But the newcomers were eyed with suspicion, scorned, and threatened by other people in surrounding areas. Lee, herself, died as the result of injuries inflicted by an angry mob in 1784. She was succeeded by James Whittaker, one of the original English Shakers whom Lee herself had named before her death. But both males and females followed in leadership roles. Joseph Meacham followed Whittaker and Lucy Wright, known as Mother Lucy, replaced Meacham after his death.

The Shakers' view of Lee as the second Christ changed over time. Although early sources portrayed them as equals, later belief held Lee more as a great prophet and model for Christianity than as a female incarnation of Christ. The Shakers' belief in God as both male and female, however, did not change. They contended that the following statement in Genesis..."Let *Us* create man in *Our* image..." meant that God was both male and female and that, based on this truth, the motherhood of God had been suppressed by 2,000 years of

Christian teaching. They believed that, in order for people to become *perfect,* they must acknowledge both the motherhood and fatherhood of God.

Development of the motherhood of God became foremost in the Shakers' work during a time in the 1840's called *Mother's Work. Holy Mother Wisdom* was believed to be a manifestation of the female in God and was also called *Mother Creation* or *Mother Warrior*, showing both the fierce and gentle sides of the female God.

Because of the teaching of Genesis that both men and women had been created in the likeness and image of God, they were considered equal in the Shaker religion. However, the Shakers agreed with other Christian religions on two points of biblical interpretation:

- They agreed that men and women had sinned through Adam and Eve and
- Women were subordinated to men because of Eve's sin, which had brought about the fall of humanity.

However, the Shakers also believed that female subordination was not final and that, through the coming of Ann Lee, male domination had been overcome and true equality had been restored.

Believing they were to be representatives of the "Kingdom of God," the Shakers set about to design the *perfect world*, making rules of governance, which to them, "mirrored the ways of heaven." They were self-sufficient in designing and building their own buildings and furniture, growing food for their tables, and providing their own clothing. While some division in tasks followed a gender line, with women working in the kitchens and dormitories and men working in the fields and outbuildings, women's work was never considered less valuable than men's.

Men, however, dominated the development of Shaker theology. But, during the period called *Mother's Work*, women were believed to be the mediums through which *Holy Mother Wisdom* spoke to the community. Based on this, most often men were thought of as the "thinkers and scholars" and women as "vehicles for religious experience."

Shakers argued that private ownership of property was a barrier to spiritual equality, so property was held in community and women had equal access. Celibate, their hearts and hands in work to God, the Shakers, both men and women, lived in a *Spiritual Family* as children of Heavenly Parents." Their daily lives were based on faith in God the Mother and God the Father. Probably nowhere else in the Christian world have women had as much equality and control as in the Shaker religion.

Today, only a few Shakers remain, and I am sad to think that such a resourceful community of people has just about vanished. Yet, they have left behind a legacy of love: empowerment for all, equality of women, and dedication to God.

Mother Goddess and Women's Culture according to Starhawk

Wicca, meaning "wise ones," is a female-centered culture based on worship of the Mother Goddess that dates back to the beginnings of civilization. Evidence of Mother Goddess has been found in numerous places around the world: in caves, in the earliest of shrines, and in the remarkable giant stone circles known as the stone henges of the British Isles. The witches of old were women who discovered healing herbs, learned the secrets of the human mind and body, eased the pain of childbirth, and cured diseases.

Persecution of these women, their worship of the Goddess, and their "craft of the wise," during the dark ages, nearly led to complete extinction of the earth-based spirituality. For the first hundred of years of Christianity, witchcraft existed peacefully alongside the *new* religion, but in the thirteenth and fourteenth centuries, during the *reign* of Pope Innocent the VIII, the persecution of witches, "as well as Jews and heretical thinkers," took the lives of over nine million people, eighty percent of whom were women. And, of these women, most were widows whose property was coveted by someone else, children who were blood relatives of witches, and midwives who were considered a threat to the male-dominated medical profession.

The propaganda of early witch trials proclaimed that witches had sold their souls to the devil, practiced obscene and disgusting rites, blighted crops, and murdered children. Mere questioning or disbelieving of this propaganda was often considered proof itself of witchcraft, or heresy.

Early scientific and literary works of women who practiced witchcraft were also nearly all destroyed by patriarchal forces, but covens of witches, groups of no more than thirteen women, preserved what was left of mythology, rituals, and knowledge of the ancient mother-centered times. Through their determination, courage, and tenacity, many women today are discovering the old religion, learning its culture, and seeking to form their own personal spirituality through the gifts of life, nature, and interaction with other women.

More important to worship within Wicca than other forms of religion are the inner feelings personal to each participant. Spiritual union to the Goddess of old is part of the Wicca religion—the Goddess being evident in all of earth, life, and nature. "Spiritual union is found in life, within nature, passion, sensuality—through being fully human, fully one's self."

The moon, as symbol of the Goddess, is of special importance to witches as it reflects the three basic stages in women's lives. The new moon represents the Maiden, the young woman who is "wild child, lady of the woods, the huntress." The full moon is the Mature Women, a sexual being, mother and nurturer, and giver of life. The dark or waning moon is the old woman, known as the Crone, who is wisdom, patroness of secrets, prophecy, divination, inspiration and power.

The Wicca Goddess is also seen as Mother Earth who sustains all growing things. She is seen as air, fire, water, and in every animal, plant, and human. She is seen as the cycles and seasons of nature, and in the mind, body, spirit, and emotions within each person. Mother Goddess is considered to be everywhere, in all that lives, and all the serves life.

Much of Wicca is strongly connected to the inner self of women. Independence, personal strength, and spirituality are highly valued. Starhawk points out, "Women have been conditioned for too long to be passive, submissive and weak."

Passion and emotion are of significant meaning to modern witches as they strive to stay in touch with their feelings, even if they are painful, "because the joy and pleasure and ecstasy available of a fully alive person make it worth occasional suffering." Anger, often considered a negative force, is considered of great value. By acknowledging, rather than denying, anger, one allows the self to know something is wrong and then do something about.

Above all else, though, Wicca values love. Their law is: "Love unto all beings." Love, Starhawk explains, is experienced in many ways. It is *falling in love*. It is mother-child love. It is love of one person for another. Love is the very personal and important relationships and interactions women have with one another. "You cannot be a witch alone, because to be a witch is to be a lover, a lover of the Goddess, and a lover of other human beings."

Within a coven, still the basic structure of Wicca, individuals come together with their own personal visions of the Goddess. Each brings a particular identity, view, and spirituality to the group and through this diversity of thought, belief, and feeling, the group receives its vitality and energy.

Rituals, formal or informal, are another important part of Wicca and, though they vary from one coven to another, are generally held in conjunction with the phases of the moon. Every ritual takes place within a circle, "a space considered to be between the worlds, the human world and the realm of the Goddess," where everyone is equal and has an opportunity to open up their intuitive and psychic abilities.

Wicca embraces not only worship, rituals, and spirituality, but it also encourages individualism, female companionship, and the work of exploring change for women in the social and political arena.

I believe that, in the years to come, more and more women will come to honor, respect, and participate in Wicca in their own personal way. Many, moved to find freedom of worship, equal rights, and acceptance of singularly developed spirituality, will welcome Wicca, and its love of life, nature, and the female ideal.

Santeria

From Africa, they came on slave ships to the Caribbean. Forcibly transported away from their homes in Southern Nigeria, Senegal, and the Guinea Coast, they were sold to the island's sugar plantation owners. Stripped of personal possessions, these Yoruba souls held fast to their one last link to freedom, their religious beliefs. While outwardly they appeared subservient, inwardly they nurtured the strength, energy, and hope of their native teachings. Not even the slavers could keep them from their thoughts, their faith, and their dreams.

Although most Africans were baptized by the Roman Catholic Church upon arrival in the Caribbean, they were not completely converted for they harbored, still, within their hearts the gods and goddesses of their Yoruba history. Even with the suppression of their native religion, the Africans found a way to blend their now secret faith into the new Catholic way. By equating their gods and goddesses, called *orishas*, to the Christian saints, they found new spiritual strength and developed what is called *Santeria*, (pronounced Saun-ta-ree'-ah).

Santeria, Spanish for "the way of the saint," a fusing of a Yoruba culture and Catholic devotion, refers to God as *Olorun,* owner of heaven. Olorun is the supreme deity, creator of the universe, and of the gods and goddesses, or orishas. Each of the orishas is associated with a particular saint. For example, St. Lazarus, patron of the sick, is known as "Babalz

Ayi." St. Barbara is "Shangs," who controls thunder, lightning, and fire. St. Anthony became "Eleggua," controller of roads and gates. St. Peter, patron of war, is called "Oggzn." The Resurrected Christ is also recognized as father of creation, source of spirituality, and called "Obatala." And these are just a few of the many hundreds of the orishas who form the basis of worship for the Santeros.

Santeros believe that each individual, even before birth, is given a destiny by the Almighty and that the orishas provide guidance, help, and energy for their life journey. Resolving the problems of everyday life, including problems of health, money, and love are requested of the orishas through divination and rituals.

Divination is usually done only by male priests called *babalawos*. The babalawos, in helping a querent with a problem, casts onto a surface a small chain that has eight pieces of shell, bone, or other materials attached to it. Each piece is shaped so that it will land facing either straight up, or down, when thrown. The possible combinations of the pieces equal two-hundred fifty-six of which each refers to a story that tells of problems that have been faced by orishas in the past—and solutions that have been found.

Rituals for the deities are filled with food, song, and dance. The orishas, the Santeros believe, must have food for sustenance just as living human beings. It is supposed that each orisha enjoys certain specials foods which may be cakes, stews, or fruit and that there is no better way to serve the orisha, or deepen the relationship, than through the symbolism of food.

Ritual sacrifices are also offered to the orishas of Santeria. Animal's blood, most commonly chicken's, sometimes sheep's, is thought to be the ultimate gift to the gods and goddesses. It is collected from the sacrificed animal and presented to the Orisha in hopes that he or she will bring good luck, purification, and forgiveness of sins to the worshipping Santeros.

Song and dance, accompanied most often by sacred *bata* drums, which provide African rhythms, surround and accompany rituals and ceremonies. Each orisha has its own individual rhythms, an *oru,* and these are played exclusively in his or her honor in calling upon them for help or to "come down" (possess an individual participating in the ritual or ceremony).

Chanting, drums, and feverish dancing are believed to invoke the orisha to "seize the head" of an individual and *speak* through him or her. In this way, the orisha delivers messages, admonitions, and advice to individual members of the Santeros' religious community. An orisha may possess one or more of those present at a ceremony and express itself not only in speech but also through dancing.

A particular orisha may assert itself as a devotee's patron, and then provide that devotee with the basic orientation in life. If the orisha *requests,* the devotee may go through an intense initiation period in which a spiritual rebirth occurs, at which time the individual is claimed to be the *true child* of the orisha. A special ceremony is then held so that the orisha may be "enthroned in the head" of the devotee and "sealed" as a permanent part of his or her personality.

Strings of colorful beads, each different and relating to a specific orisha, are worn by a Santeros for protection. An initiate, who is often given a male and female orisha for a mother and a father by the Santeros community, wears the particular beads of these deities along with those of various others. Beads, floral fragrances, and embroidered costumes are all a part of the power objects that belong to the orishas.

I found readings on Santeria and a presentation by Ana Arroyo, a EMU professor, quite fascinating. Despite attempts by the Catholic Church to indoctrinate the African slaves and suppress their own native religion, they could not succeed. Too powerful were the deities of old, too much a part of the Yoruba cultural history. The slavers could take away the freedom of the Yoruba people's bodies but never, the yearnings, beliefs, and needs of their souls.

Conflicting Images of God in Early Christianity

"The absence of feminine symbolism of God marks Judaism, Christianity, and Islam in striking contrast to the world's other religious traditions, whether in Egypt, Babylonia, Greece, and Rome or Africa, Polynesia, India, and North America," says Elaine H. Pagels. She adds that although Christianity added the Trinitarian terms to the Jewish description of God, the divine three became both masculine, Father and Son, and sexless, the Spirit. Nowhere was God the Mother to be found. Mixed texts, identified as both Jewish and Christian Gnostic works, were attacked and condemned as heretical nearly sixteen hundred years earlier. Still, varied attitudes toward the existence of God the Mother emerged.

Written on papyrus and hidden in large clay jars since circa A.D. 100-150, these texts revealed the belief in the feminine God: God the Mother, Mother the Creator, and Mother the Spirit, mostly characterized in these sources in three primary ways.

The first characterization, as described by Valentinus, a certain poet and teacher, is that God is essentially indescribable, but suggests that the divine can be imagined as a Dyad of two elements, one called the Source, the Primal Father, and the other Silence, the Mother of all things. Followers of Valentinus appeal to Her as *Grace* or *divine eternal Grace*. Sometimes they pray to her, as *Mother* for protection: "...Thou enthroned with God, eternal, mystical Silence."

Marcus, a disciple of Valentinus, asserts that, "when Moses began his account of creation, he mentioned the Mother of all things at the very beginning when he said, "In the beginning, God created the heavens and the earth." For the *beginning* (in Greek, the Feminine *Arche*) refers to the divine Mother, the source of the cosmic elements.

I think it is an interesting concept to consider: Mother of all things, as the source of all life, the *beginning* of all things, God the Mother. Thinking creatively, it is possible to imagine that God and She are Mother of all and guide to the Father in creating the world. Their conversation might have gone like this:

"All is too silent." God the Mother speaks quietly, her voice almost grieving. "We must change all this, create a place and time and life for others. We must give them love, teach them to share, and above all—"

"A free will," God the Father speaks. "Give them rules to follow. Teach them to obey. Have them learn respect...create them in our own images."

"You are right. They must have all those teachings, opportunities, and blessings, many blessings, and the knowledge that they may turn to us, their Parents, in love. And we will forever be there for them." God the Mother is smiling, imagining the future.

I also find the second characterization of the divine Mother as Holy Spirit an interesting idea. In the *Secret Book of John,* as he goes out after the crucifixion and encounters a mystical vision of the Trinity, he says, "As I was grieving, the heavens were opened, and the whole creation shone with an unearthly light, and the universe was shaken. I was afraid. And behold, a unity in three forms appeared to me. And I wondered, how can a unity have three forms?" The vision then replies, "I am the One who is with you always. I am the Father. I am the Mother. I am the Son."

In the *Secret Book,* the author looks to the Hebrew term for spirit, *ruah*, a feminine word and concludes, that the feminine person joined with Father and Son must be the Mother: "The image of the invisible virginal perfect spirit, she became the mother of the all, for she existed before them all. In the secret *Gospel to the Hebrews,* Jesus speaks of, "my Mother, the Spirit." And in yet another text, the *Gospel of Phillips,* the virgin birth is referred to as the mysterious union of the two divine powers, the Father of all with the Holy Spirit.

A third characterization of the divine Mother is as *Wisdom*. Early scholars suggested, "Wisdom bears two connotations. First, she bestows the Spirit that makes mankind wise. Second, she is a creative power, the first universal creator. God the Father was speaking to her when he proposed to make mankind in His image—their image: Father, Mother, unity, Root of all things."

While Pagels explains that to look for the historical reasons why these Gnostic writings were suppressed is an extremely difficult proposition, but the work is progressing. Why were certain ideas classified as heretical while others as orthodox? The research is still in its early stages, but it is most feasible to imagine that much of the writings about God as Mother were suppressed because "the recognition of mankind as male and female bore explosive social possibility of women acting on an equal basis with men in positions of authority and leadership."

Were the Gnostic texts buried out of fear? Or were they buried so that one day they would be rediscovered, the *truths* about God the Mother reevaluated, and the future, as well as history, rewritten? Perhaps, a future great granddaughter and other women of her time will find the answers to these remarkable and thought provoking questions.

Gathering in the Garden of Eden

Coralie Cederna Johnson

Is the story of Adam and Eve truth or fiction? History or myth? It depends on whom one asks. For many, it is history; for others it is myth. But truth or fiction, history or myth, the tale of what happened in the Garden of Eden has affected nearly every Christian woman's life.

> "...God created man in his own image...then the Lord God said, "it is not good that the man should be alone; I will make him a helper fit for him"...so the Lord God caused a deep sleep to fall upon the man, and while he slept, took one of his ribs...and the rib, which the Lord God had taken from the man, he made into a woman and brought her to the man..."
>
> Did God say, "You shall not eat of any tree of the garden"? And the woman said to the serpent, "We may eat of the fruit of the trees of the garden, but God said, 'You shall not eat of the fruit of the tree which is in the midst of the garden, lest you die.' And the serpent said to the woman, "You will not die. For God knows that, when you eat of it, your eyes will be opened, and you will be like God, knowing good and evil." Then she took of its fruit and ate; and she also gave some to her husband, and he ate" (Genesis 1:27, 2:18-22, 3:1-6).

The Creation Story has been told again and again and, while in the past centuries few women dared to openly question the validity, veracity, and consequences of this story, feminist writers today are speaking out.

Elaine Pagels writes in her recent book, *Adam, Eve, and the Serpent*, "As I investigated Jewish and Christian sources, I found myself fascinated with the story of Adam, Eve, and the serpent, written down by members of Hebrew tribes about three thousand years ago, and probably told for generations before that. I had always assumed that this archaic story wielded an extraordinary influence upon western culture, but as my work progressed I was surprised to discover how complex and extensive its effect has been" (Pagels xix).

Banishment from the Garden of Eden is seen as the result of Eve's sin and evil. She is blamed for the edicts of the Creation Story's God who promised that man would suffer and toil; that woman would suffer in childbirth; and that woman would be subject to man. Negative attitudes toward women, stereotyping them as weak, have emerged unconsciously from the Creation Story. Many, in our culture today, believe that suffering, death, and disease are all a result of sin and so we (women) blame ourselves for things that happen that perhaps are not our fault. And often guilt results (Pagels with Moyer).

Intrigued with Pagels' hypothesis and discussions which followed in a Women and Religion course led by Professor Bonnie Brereton at Eastern Michigan University, I became curious to learn more about the effects of the Creation Story on women's lives today and so set about to conduct further research. I quickly discovered that many feminist writers share Pagels' views that nearly every Christian woman who had been told a Creation

Story in her early childhood, has been negatively affected by its lessons learned in formative years and, as an adult, is dealing with its ramifications.

> "The tale of Adam, Eve, the rib, the apple and the fall is the most fully described story in women's writings. We know this story. It was engraved on the canvases, storybook pages, and memories of our childhoods. Eve was morally weak and more susceptible to the wiles of the devil than the man was. She was the first to surrender to temptation. She violated God's law and then seduced the man. It was her sexuality that caused the downfall of all humankind."
>
> The information about Eve that women pick up in their childhoods is simple and very clear. [It] convinced us of our "proper place" as women, of the qualities that define the essence of womanhood, and of the pain and suffering that is the lot of a woman's life. The image imprinted on women's imaginations is clear: A male God created Adam in his image. Eve was merely an afterthought. She was to keep the man company, to service him sexually, and to keep the garden neat and clean, while Adam and God carried on the important business of running the world (Reilly 110-111).

The realm of blame transferred to women from Eve, through the telling and retelling of the Creation Story, ranges from abstruse accusation to certain condemnation. Not only do the lessons learned by women seek to convince them of their proper place as second-class citizens, accuse them of being morally weak, and charge them with being sexually promiscuous, but they also castigate them as corrupt. Eve—woman—because she incarnates inferior energies, becomes a stereotypical source of evil. The Church Fathers propagate a suitable mythology. "Women, do you not know that you are Eve? You are the devil's gateway. How easily you destroyed man, the image of God' [Tertullian]" (Kolbenschlag 184).

As I reflected on these perplexing ideas, my own childhood experience of the Creation Story, its negative connotations, and impact on my life came into focus. It became important to compare my concepts, feelings, and attitudes with other women. So I decided to ask other women the questions I had asked myself. I asked when they had first heard the story of Adam and Eve, their age at the telling, and what their religion had been. Had Original Sin been a part of the story, did they think Eve had sinned and, if so, how had they felt about it? Did they accept the story as truth or did they question the teaching.

I asked them to recall their first remembrance, understanding, and visualization of God and whether their perceptions today differed. As adults, did they believe the story to be history or myth? Did they still support their childhood religion?

In further regard to their current religions, or non-religions, did they feel their religion was male-based, respectful to women, and offer the same equality to women as to men? And finally, I asked them to include any cultural history, special notes, or views that are part of their religious beliefs today.

Feminist writers, I found, are not the only female voices straining to be heard. Christian women, taking another looking at the Creation Story, remember how they accepted it with blind faith, trust, and, in some cases, guilt, disappointment, and anger. And, they are anxious to revisit old issues, evaluate their influences, and discuss them as a basis of their current experiences, choices, and beliefs within their religions.

Of various age, race, and religion (Baptist, Roman Catholic, Pentecostal, Methodist, African Methodist Episcopal Zion, Assembly of God), the essence of these Christian women's answers proved a common core. All had heard the Creation Story, when they were very young, ages five to eight years old. And most had accepted it as history, since adults in authoritative religious positions, whom, as children, they would not have doubted, had told them it was true.

All of the women believed that Eve had sinned, though even as children, most wondered why Adam was not as much to blame as she. Many blamed the serpent for tempting Eve. Expressions of anger, guilt, and disappointment followed: "When I was about five, my great-grandmother told me that, because Eve had sinned, women had painful periods and that was the price we had to pay," wrote Karen S., African Methodist Episcopal Zion.

Roman Catholic women responded in the following terms of frustration: "I felt not guilt, nor disappointment, but anger!" said Jacquie, who had entered a Catholic convent at age fifteen, but later left to marry and have a family. Connie stated, "I felt really upset that Eve was blamed. I wished it were the man who had given in to the serpent, so girls wouldn't be blamed for Original Sin. I felt very unhappy that I had been born "bad" with Original Sin on my soul. I was a sinner before, or at the moment of birth. It didn't seem fair." And Joan, who no longer supports the Roman Catholic Church, said, "The Original Sin story was the "original" attempt at conditioning women "to know their place as second to men. It was a sin to be curious and explore that curiosity."

Debbi, who asserts she has "fallen away" from her childhood Temple Methodist Church, said, "Adam was wrong, weak, and didn't stand up for what he thought. He let Eve do the work, the thinking, and the decision making and dumped the guilt on her."

For most, regardless of race, the childhood conception of God was that of a powerful white male clothed in flowing robes of white trimmed in gold, who lived in an immense temple somewhere up in the clouds, where he sat upon a golden throne. They admitted that their religions today are male-based and that they are acutely aware of disrespect and inequality for women within those religions.

"Women do not have a respectful or equal place in religion. We're always in a one-down position, it seems—in supportive roles. Why couldn't a woman celebrate Mass? The message is that there is something fundamentally inferior about women," stated Carrie, a Roman Catholic.

"I am equal to any man in God's eyes. Some men don't seem to understand that, but I no longer care. What God thinks matters far more to me," another Roman Catholic said.

An African-American woman said of her Pentecostal religion, "Women have a respectful place in my religion, but they are not equal to men."

Another African-American woman agreed, "Yes, there is some respect, but women do not have as equal a place as men in my Baptist religion, either."

"Women equal to men in religion? Hell, no! All western religions are male-based and uphold a disrespect towards women," spouted one of the women who no longer attends regular church.

"In Christianity, Jesus honored women and their opinions. In my church, they have forgotten this fact. There is respect for women in my religion, but not in the church I attend," stated a woman who has been a life-long member of the African Methodist Episcopal Zion Church.

"I was raised Roman Catholic. Today, I am a religion of one where women have as equal a place as men do," stated Joan, who occasionally takes her mother to Sunday Mass, but does not participate herself.

It is fascinating to note that although most of these women, in speaking of their earliest memories of God, the Creation Story, and how these things have molded their thoughts, actions, and understandings of religion, or non-religion, today, have never met one another, their stories show a common bond of sisterhood in shared history, strength of spirit, and determination:

> "I first heard the story of Adam and Eve in Temple Methodist Church when I was four and learned about sin from attending the Catholic Church with my best friend. I did not understand how Eve could have sinned as she was only showing curiosity. I do not like organized religion, but occasionally attend the Unitarian Church."
>
> Debbi
> No specific religion

> "I read this story in *Children's Bible Stories,* when I was five and remember wondering why Eve was punished for thinking for herself. My grandfather, who had a doctorate in Theology, encouraged us to think for ourselves, so early on I questioned the teachings of this story, which today I consider a myth.
>
> There are still very strong undertones of African beliefs and traditions that have shaped many African-American's understanding of Christianity and their concept of Original Sin. As a Black person, I question more the gospel. When I was a child I thought of God as the Voice in the Flame, or the Voice in the Whirlwind—the Holy Spirit—that could come down and possess people so that they would shout and dance for joy. Today I still visualize God as the Voice in the Whirlwind. I believe that all things are inhabited by the Voice or Will of God."
>
> Karen
> African Methodist Episcopal Zion

"Even though the Creation Story seemed unbelievable to me at age six, I was sure that nuns and priests would not lie. Still, I hoped they might be, at least partially, mistaken. It seemed odd to me that God would put these two people he loved in paradise, allow them to be tempted, and then take it (paradise) all away, with no second chances.

It was a worry to me to learn from the nuns that, if someone died before being baptized, they would go straight to hell for something they didn't do. I often questioned the whole business of Original Sin and prayed that God, who was good and kind, wouldn't hate me for questioning.

I really loved God a lot and still do. And I feel God loves me back, questions, doubts, and all."

Connie
Roman Catholic

"When I was five years old, I learned of Adam and Eve and the serpent in the Pentecostal Church. I never questioned the validly of this story because I trusted my minister. I believed that both Adam and Eve had sinned, but I blamed the serpent because it took advantage of Eve.

My first understanding of God was when I looked at nature for the first time. I knew man could not have created flowers, fruit, rain, snow and clouds. I have always thought of God as a presence, a spirit with no face."

Cheryl
Pentecostal

"I was six when I heard the story in Catholic grade school. I didn't think Adam had sinned, but accepted on "faith" that women were weak, kind of dumb and at fault. I thought it was history, but now I question the teaching.
Today I do not believe in an individual as God. My religion is private, personal, and self-taught."

Joan
A Religion of One

"Growing up, I heard the story of Adam and Eve in Catholic catechism class. I was about six. I blamed the serpent for enticing Eve, but I still felt Eve was at fault, which made me feel sad about the apparent weakness of women in the story.

I do believe in Original Sin, or at least collective sin we all participate in and need to be forgiven for. I'm comfortable with the teaching of the Catholic Church, but I also feel it's male-based (human imperfection in the Institution of the Catholic Church). Women are in supportive roles only.

My childhood image of God, as in Michelangelo's painting, does not fit for me today as I find it limiting and inaccurate. However, a woman-image doesn't seem to fit, either, and I can't wrap my mind's eye around an "all powerful force." Maybe that's why Jesus Christ came to us, in part, to have a visual image, an actual divine person with whom to connect. Now, I usually pray to Jesus when I need help.

It does feel as though women are viewed as the weaker sex, and maybe this dates back to Eve."

Carrie
Roman Catholic

"I was seven or eight when I heard the story of Adam and Eve. I believed there were *good guys* and *bad guys*—serpent and Eve were the *bad guys*. I did not question the teaching. It was as the preacher said and it had to be true as the preacher was my grandfather.

I am comfortable with my religion and feel women are respected but do not feel that women have as equal a place in my religion as men do.

My first understanding of God was that God was all knowing, all benevolent, and creator of all things. I pictured him as Charlton Heston's "Moses." I realize now that God is much more complex than I first learned. But, in my most secret moments, I still picture him looking like Mr. Heston's "Moses."

Sharon
Baptist

"As a child, I was certain that the story of Adam and Eve was historically true, but as an adult, I see it could be a myth. But it doesn't matter. At seven years old, I felt angry that Eve had sinned. However, I also felt that Adam, Eve, and the serpent all shared the blame.

My understanding of God took a big step when I was fifteen. I read a book on the Trinity and it described how the beautiful Holy Spirit is the love the Father and Son share. I was in a convent.

My adult understanding of Eve and her sin is that I participated somehow in her decision. I do not know today if that is how Adam and Eve were created or if the story is solely symbolical. I do believe an intelligence is behind the creation of billions of stars and billions of people, and that an intelligent *person*, if capable of designing the universe, could create humans, or—at a point in their evolution—touch them, with divinity.

> Sometimes men in the Church seem not to recognize how fantastically valuable women are. But God? He (if *he* is the correct noun) gave women their beauty, intelligence, courage, honesty, compassion, and heart. He knows us and that's what counts."
>
> Jacquie
> Roman Catholic

Only Norma's personal account differs greatly from the other women's. Interestingly, her husband, a preacher, offered her advice as she completed the survey questions.

> "I have never questioned the teachings of the Creation Story. It is God's word and God's word is truth.
>
> We can't change the fact that Eve listened to the serpent, but I guess as women we would like to think it would have been Adam. Eve gave the fruit of the tree to Adam. This is fact. We may not like it, but Eve was a woman who listened to the serpent and put God's warning aside.
>
> I feel that women have both a respectful and equal place in my religion and I do not feel my religion is male-based. The bible states, 'God sent His son.'
>
> Norma
> Assembly of God

All of these women through their personal accounts, whether single, married or divorced; aged thirty, forty, fifty or sixty-five; of various races—with the exception of Norma—attest to first-hand experiences of spiritual suffering brought about through early conditioning by Christian religious stories.

> "Religious stories hold within them tremendous power. Centuries ago it was men who wrote down and then gathered together into sacred books the stories that were circulating by word of mouth throughout the Hebrew and early Christian communities. These storytellers, writers, and then translators were all rooted in a culture and society that worshipped God the father and thus preferred men. Their choice of what was meaningful and to be preserved carried this dominant male perspective" (Reilly 99).

That we women grew up with the guilt, disappointment, and anger at Eve's *seduction* by the serpent does not mean that we must continue to be seduced by our own religions. "Visiting the Garden of Eden in the days of the Women's Movement," Phyllis Tribble notes in *Eve and Adam: Genesis 2-3 Reread,* "we need no longer accept the traditional exegesis of Genesis 2-3. Rather than legitimating the patriarchal culture from which it comes, the myth places that culture under judgment. And thus it functions to liberate, not to enslave" (Tribble 81).

History or myth, interpretations of the Creation Story have sentenced most Christian women to a term of self-doubt, guilt, and anger. It has allowed men, who fear the loss of their own unearned control and power, to cast women into subservient roles within their religions. But women can commute their own sentences by gathering together in the Garden of Eden and realizing their shared strength of knowledge, history, and wisdom can be a powerful tool in creating change. They can recognize, renew, and redefine their early attitudes and faith, overturning the messages, visions, and teachings of guilt, disrespect, and inequality.

Healing, growth, and development of women's self-perception, self-love, and spirituality are available to women who realize that the freedom to move onward and upward in our communities, our religions, and our own *gardens of the world* is there for the taking.

Who was Agnes Gonxha Bojaxhiu? ~ Coralie Cederna Johnson

(Born in Skopje, Macedonia in 1910, Agnes was born to a devout Roman Catholic family. She was a teacher of history and a nun, before she became known as Mother Teresa, founder of the Order of the Missionaries of Charity.)

Some find religion in silent prayer and devotion. Agnes Gonxha Bojaxhiu, having been raised by religious parents, certainly did. But it was the active role in helping others she took throughout life that brought her to find her true religious expression of love.

In 1919, when Agnes was only eight years old, her father died suddenly, and she became even closer to her mother than she had before his death. Following her mother's lead, Agnes learned to care for others; to be responsible for the health and care of the poor, and to commit one's self to being charitable to all.

Her mother, Drana Bojaxhiu, although not wealthy, began to invite the most disadvantaged families in the city to come dine with her family. She told Agnes, "My child, never eat a single mouthful unless you are sharing it with others." And when Agnes asked who the people eating with them were, her mother responded, "Some of them are our relations, but all of them are our people."

So it was at an early age that Agnes came to understand the plight of poverty-stricken people of her city and how many needed help with the most basic elements of life: food, clothing, and shelter. She also knew, she would one day, do all she could to help others. And she did. She found ways to bring bread to those living in poverty; medicine for the ill; and spiritual love for the lost and lonely.

But she was never lonely. Her daily goals of caring for others carried her through periods of life that could have been dark. But there was light. Through her kindness and giving nature, she created light in a world of longing for so many.

As a young girl, Agnes attended a convent-run school, where her class was taken on a pilgrimage to the chapel of the Madonna of Letnice on Black Mountain in Skopje. And it was there, at age twelve, she first felt a calling to a religious life. Six years later, in 1928, an 18-year-old Agnes Bojaxhiu decided to become a nun and set off for Ireland to join the Loreto Sisters of Dublin. There she took the name of Sister Mary Teresa after Saint Thérèse of Lisieux.

Sister Mary Teresa was to eventually become known as Mother Teresa. But before that, she was a history teacher in India for seventeen years. Her convent sent her to Calcutta, where she was assigned to teach at Saint Mary's High School for Girls, a school run by the Loreto Sisters and dedicated to teaching girls from the city's poorest families. There she dedicated herself to making the girls' lives better through education.

Some years later, she was named Mother Teresa by her convent and went on to found the Order of the Missionaries of Charity, devoting her life to care for the poor and the sick. Her order developed hospice help for the dying, greatly relieving the pain and suffering of many.

What I especially love about Mother Teresa's devoted life and actions is that she did not judge anyone. That was not her mission, nor was it of any assistance in a life of giving to others. Mother Teresa's strength of character, her spirit, and her motivation to help all, live on. She spoke of forgiveness and kindness no matter what occurred. She spoke of the importance of happiness and helping others. She reminded her followers to give their best always, whether it was appreciated, or not. In the end, she pointed out, our lives and all we do is between God and us, and that is what matters.

What greater religious tenets, works, and beliefs can there be? Her concern for humankind encompassed all. Mother Teresa's legacy is one of pure inspiration—a love and life to aspire to.

Healing the Heart

Coralie Cederna Johnson

I want to tell you a story about how the gift of understanding and belief in God came to me at an early age. That was when my Aunt Santina introduced me to the miracles of everyday life, love, and living each day to the fullest. But all of this began with an accident that led to a terrible tragedy for our family.

I was four years old. My cousin Joanne was seven. We had become inseparable companions in our short years of life. But I would soon learn the lesson of loss, unexpected grief, and overwhelming heartache. But I would also learn that endings have a way of becoming beginnings, when you have someone with whom to share troubled times.

My cousin Joanne, with her parents, Aunt Santina and Uncle Mike, lived just three doors down the block. And even though she was a grown up seven and I was only four, we were the best of friends.

When she went off to school that fall, I thought I'd die without her. I gave up trying to count the long hours of each weekday, convinced that the weekend would never arrive. But somehow the days ticked slowly away until we could once again be together, make up for lost time, and play our favorite games in my back yard.

But then something terrible happened.

We'd been warned not to play piggyback. Caught in the act, we'd been told it was too dangerous. But the older kids in the neighborhood all did it. As soon as our parents were out of sight, Joanne would boost me up on her shoulders and away we'd go, wobbling, pitching, and stumbling until we'd tumble to the ground, giggling so hard we could barely pick ourselves up again.

One Saturday afternoon, as Joanne strutted about the yard with me on her back, our laughter sent us sailing with such speed around the front of the house that we nearly fell headlong into Mom's Snowball bushes. Joanne tried to stop the fall by taking a quick step backward, but her feet got tangled and she ran straight into the sharp corner of our front porch, jabbing her side and hurling us into a heap.

I thought, at first, she was still laughing. But when I tried to roll her over, I could see she wasn't. She was crying. I begged her not to go home, but she didn't seem to hear me. I watched her limp along down the block, holding her side and sobbing.

I hoped she would come back after supper. I waited and waited, but she didn't come.

I waited for her the next day again, but she still didn't come.

At our house, a strange thing was going on. My parents seemed to have a secret. They would often whisper to each other, and then stop when I came into the room.

Finally on Monday evening, Mom told me Joanne was sick. She had a badly ruptured appendix.

"Is Joanne better yet?" I kept asking my mother on Tuesday, but each time the answer was no.

On Tuesday night, I heard the phone ring, then Mom's voice sounding sad.

When she hung up the phone, she looked at me and said, "Coralie, come into the living room. Let's sit down. I want to talk to you."

She took my hand and led me to the sofa in the living room.

"That was Aunt Santina on the phone," Mom continued, looking at me in an odd way.

"Is Joanne better?" I asked.

"Coralie," she hesitated, "Joanne isn't going to get better." She put her arm around me as we sat of the sofa. "She's gone to heaven. She's one of God's special little angels now. She was very sick, you know, and now she won't be in pain anymore."

"She's going to be an angel? Then I won't see her anymore?" I'd seen picture of angels in my aunt's prayer book and tried hard to imagine what that meant.

In my restless dreams that night, I could see Joanne's face. Her short, soft curls spilled out from underneath the brim of her favorite hand-knit Scandinavian cap, forming a soft golden halo around her sky-blue eyes. But when I reached out and tried to touch her, I couldn't, because she was an angel, floating in heaven with all God's other special angels. Her face was happy, but I woke up crying and sad. I would never see my friend again.

"Can I go to the funeral?" I asked Mom.

"No, dear, you are too little. Only the grown-ups will be there," Mom answered, her eyes red-rimmed.

Standing in our back yard on the day of Joanne's funeral, I could see the mourners in black walk slowly in the cold drizzling rain from their cars to Aunt Santina's back door, then disappear inside. I stood silently watching until there were no more people, only empty cars. I felt small, chilled, and alone.

I would never see Joanne again. I didn't have anyone to play with. Even when Mom read bedtime stories to me, I felt sad and lonely. All winter long, I thought about Joanne, dreamed about her, and sometimes even pretended that she was with me...just invisible.

There were hushed conversations I sometimes overheard during those winter months. "I don't know how she's ever going to get through this," my father said to my mother, referring to his sister, my aunt. "She hardly eats enough to keep a bird alive. And she cries all the time."

I worried about her. I missed Joanne, but I missed my favorite aunt, too. It was a long winter.

When spring came, I stood at our northerly dining room window, looking off across the street to the field where topsy-turvy patches of burnt brown Indian tobacco, wild wheat, and weeping white milkweed waved invitingly in the sun. I wished Joanne were there so we could go exploring for buttercups, birds, and berries.

"I think the strawberries are ripe," Mom said brightly, interrupting my daydreams. "How would you like to go and see?"

"By myself?" I'd never been across the street alone before.

Mom hesitated, then went to the kitchen sink, rinsed out her little tin measuring cup, dried it on a blue and white striped kitchen towel and handed it to me. "By yourself. It's time you learned to cross alone. I'll walk you to the edge of the street. But when you come back, remember to look both ways for cars, just like we've talked about." She pressed the tin cup into my hand, smiled, and walked me to the street.

Excited about my adventure, I looked back only once to see if my mother was still watching me. But she'd gone back inside. So, I made my way through the waist-high waving grass, stooping now and again to press grass and leaves aside to look for red berries.

Suddenly, I came upon a huge boulder hidden in the grass. Bigger than me and polished by years of sun, snow, and rain, it had a fragrance all its own. I breathed in the heady smell, so like the lovely shoreline of a summer lake. I ran my hands over the pocked surface, found a notch halfway up just big enough for the toe of my white sandal and scrambled up.

Stretching out on its cool surface, like a tricky toad, I moved not at all, blending into my surroundings so convincingly that the orange and black Monarch butterflies fluttering by could not tell me from the rock. The breath of their wings tickled my knees as they landed, then took off again.

To the musical trill of a meadowlark nesting nearby, I gazed up toward the serene sapphire sky, letting my thoughts float along with the puffy white clouds overhead as they scudded slowly along, taking the shapes of dancing dogs, circus elephants, and...angels, like Joanne.

Spring came and went. Then, one day in early summer, the phone rang.

"Coralie, that was Aunt Santina. She wants you to come for a visit. How would you like that?" Mom asked, obviously pleased.

"You mean I can go alone?" I'd been across the street, but never on a visit by myself.

"Yes, I think you're big enough now," Mom said.
I was thrilled. Not only was I going on a visit by myself, but I would finally get to see my special aunt again, too.

Mom slipped my white embroidered pinafore over my head, then hooked each of my long curls around her forefinger and brushed it into a perfect bobbing spiral. She polished my white sandals, gave me a pair of white anklets to pull on and gave my face a few swipes with a warm wet washcloth that smelled sweetly of Sweetheart Soap.

Excited, I hopped along down the sidewalk to Aunt Santina's house, counting the sections of cement and carefully skipping over each crack.

I slowed when I reached the pruned entrance to the yard and walked like a lady to the back door. There, behind the screen door, stood my aunt waiting. But she had a strange look on her face. Was something wrong? I didn't know what to do. We just stood there looking at each other for what seemed like a long time, until I began to wonder if I should go back home.

But then she opened the door, stepped out, and looked off over my head.

"The wrens have come back," she said wistfully, pointing to the tiny birdhouse hung in the maple tree just outside her kitchen window. "They are such hard workers. Never stop from dawn 'til dusk." Her thoughts seemed far away as she watched the little brown birds flitting back and forth from her garden to their house.

"They're so tiny!" I exclaimed.

"Yes, they are, tiny but hardy," she answered, turning and walking toward her backyard garden.

"Look at all those sad little faces," she said more to herself than to me as we examined clusters of bright lavender, purple, and yellow pansies peering up at us.

I followed her from flower to flower enjoying the colors of her garden. Grouped in perfect little patches were pink carnations, white Shasta daisies, and blue bachelor buttons, bordered by orange nasturtiums, yellow four-o'clocks, and red moss roses. At each new plant, she stopped and pulled away dead leaves and stems.

"Your flowers are so pretty. I love the colors," I said, hoping to cheer her up, hoping she would look at me. She didn't seem to remember I was there.

"Yes, the garden is comforting," she replied. Her voice was somber, her thoughts far away, her eyes clouded over. She seemed lost from me.

But after several seconds, she finally spoke again. "Come," she said looking off across the garden, "I have something to show you."

I followed her to the far corner of the garden. "These are new this year," she said pointing to a clump of pink and white flowers.

I walked over to get a closer look. Here grew the most amazing flowering plant I had ever seen, abundant green branches weighted down with small pink heart-shaped flowers, each split down the middle by a white pendulum.

"They're called Bleeding Hearts," she said, studying the flowers.

"They look like broken hearts," I said. Just like mine, I thought.

She didn't respond at once. I began to wonder if she'd ever look at me.

"Yes, dear." I heard grief in her voice. "They are one of God's little miracles. He knows when our hearts are sad and has given us a symbol of His understanding to remind us that He understands our pain."

"Can we pick them?" I thought how pretty they'd look in a vase.

She fell silent...thinking. I looked up at her and tried to see her eyes, but they were still turned from me. However, she seemed to be making an important decision. I wondered what it was.

"I have a better idea," she finally answered. "We'll let them be for now. Then we can come back each day and see how they've grown."

With this, she summoned up her courage and turned to look me squarely in the eyes. She forced herself to smile through her tears. "Would you like to come and visit me again," she asked, "tomorrow?"

"And we can walk in the garden again?" I asked.

"We certainly can, Coralie. We can walk in the garden...together," my aunt answered.

Then, as she reached out and took my tiny hand in hers, I felt the wonderful warmth of her touch ease the pain of my broken heart. And I knew everything was going to be all right. I had thought Joanne was lost forever, but there in the garden I felt the miracle of her presence, her memory blessed by the Bleeding Hearts.

Our visits to the garden became the most important events in our lives during that summer. As hand-in-hand we shared the beauty, peace, and joy of God's wonders, we also held Joanne silently within our grieving hearts. And through this gentle companionship of love and hope and grace, our hearts, at last, began to heal.

* * *

And yes, I still believe in miracles. I see, hear, and feel them happening every day. And I rejoice in the love of the God I know and trust, the God whose higher power helped my family and me find our way out of deep sadness and into a place of peace.

I am a woman of faith. And I embrace and honor others and their individual religions, beliefs, and faiths. There is much to be learned from each other as we work to make our lives, communities, and the world a better place to live. Blending our resources for the good of all is best accomplished when we reach out and listen to each other. As I've learned over and over again, listening and understanding without judging is the most enduring gift one can give another. Thank you for listening to my words...and God bless.

Sources: Reflections on Women & Religion

Divine Mosaic ~ Images of the Sacred Other, The. Ed. Theresa King. Yes International Publications. St. Paul, MN. 1994.

Antiga. "The Goddess in Me." Divine Mosaic ~ Images of the Sacred Other, The. Ed. Theresa King. Yes International Publications. St. Paul, MN. 1994.

Banks, Carolyn. "The Virgin of Polish Hill." Divine Mosaic ~ Images of the Sacred Other, The. Ed. Theresa King. Yes International Publications. St. Paul, MN. 1994.

Haddad, Yvonne Yazbeck. "Islam, Women, and Revolution in Twentieth-Century Arab Thought." Women and Religion. Course Pack. Ed. Brereton, Professor Bonnie. Eastern Michigan University. 1997.

Kinsley, David. "Sacred Female Imagery and Women's Religious Experience in Hinduism." Women and Religion. Course Pack. Ed. Brereton, Professor Bonnie. Eastern Michigan University. 1997.

Mother Theresa: "Do it anyway." Online 10 Aug 2013. Available: http://prayerfoundation.org/mother_teresa_do_it_anyway.htm

Mother Teresa Biography. Online. 10 Aug. 2013. Available: http://www.biography.com/people/mother-teresa-9504160

Setta, Susan M. "When Christ Is a Woman: Theology and Practice in the Shaker Tradition," Women and Religion. Course Pack. Ed. Brereton, Professor Bonnie. Eastern Michigan University. 1997.

Siou, Lily. "Voice of God, Mother of Life." Divine Mosaic ~ Images of the Sacred Other, The. Ed. Theresa King. Yes International Publications. St. Paul, MN. 1994.

Starhawk. "Witchcraft and Women's Culture." Women and Religion. Course Pack. Ed. Brereton, Professor Bonnie. Eastern Michigan University. 1997.

Win, Wawokiya. "Our Grandfather The Great Spirit." Divine Mosaic ~ Images of the Sacred Other, The. Ed. Theresa King. Yes International Publications. St. Paul, MN. 1994.

Nunez, Luis. Santeria: a practical guide to Afro-Caribbean Magic. Spring Publications, 1992.

Pagels, Elaine H. Pagels, "What Became of God the Mother? Conflicting Images of God in Early Christianity." Online. Available 5 Aug 2013. http://www.jstor.org/discover/10.2307/3173448?uid=3739728&uid=2129&uid=2&uid=70&uid=4&uid=3739256&sid=21102524768997. The University of Chicago Press. 1976.

Pagels, Elaine H. Pagels, Gnostic Gospels, The. Vintage; 1st Vintage Books. 1989.

Sources: Gathering in the Garden of Eden

Book of Genesis, The. Chapters 1:27, 2:18-22, 3:1-6, (Revised Standard Version)

Johnson, Coralie. Survey and interviews conducted with Christian women. May-June 1997.

Kolbenschlag, Madonna. Kiss Sleeping Beauty Good-Bye. (New York: Harper & Row, 1982), 184.

Pagels, Elaine. Adam, Eve, and the Serpent. (New York: Vintage, 1988), xix.

Pagels, Elaine with Bill Moyer. Video interview re: Adam, Eve, and the Serpent.

Reilly, Patricia Lynn. A God Who Looks Like Me. (New York: Ballantine, 1995), 99, 110, 111.

Tribble, Phyllis. "Eve and Adam: Genesis 2-3 Reread." Andover Newton Quarterly 13, (March, 1973), 81.

Literature Review: Sacrificial Offerings

AYLWARD, GLADYS (1904-1970): *Missionary to China.*

Kiefer, James. "Gladys Aylward, Missionary to China." Online. 26 Jul. 2013 Available: http://justus.anglican.org/resources/bio/73.html. *Gladys Aylward discusses the difficulties she encountered on her missionary travels.*

Swift, Catherine. "Gladys Aylward. The Courageous English Missionary Who's Life Defied All Expectations." Women of Faith. Bethany House Publishers. 1984. *This book describes Gladys Aylward's life as a young woman, her call to become a missionary in China and her experiences in that country.*

Wellman, Sam. "Heroes of History." Online: www.heroesofhistory.com/page46.html. *This biographical sketch of Gladys Aylward discusses her missionary work and reaction to Hollywood's portrayal of her in the film INN OF THE SIXTH HAPPINESS.*

BESANT, ANNIE (1847-1933): *Christian minister's wife & convert to Theosophy.*

Johnson, Jane. "Annie Besant, Heretic." http://womenshistory.about.com/od/freethought/a/annie_besant.htm. *This biographical article discusses Annie Besant's role as a minister's wife, her break from Christianity, and her conversion to Theosophy.*

Malafaia, Teresa de Ataide. "The Canon Reconsidered and Annie Besant's Marginality." Online. 26 Jul. 2013 Available: http://www.victorianweb.org/authors/besant/besant1.html. *This article questions the importance of Besant's works.*

Malafaia, Teresa de Ataide. "Annie Besant's Shifting Identity and Fin-de-Siecle Culture (2): In Search of an Identity." Online. 26 Jul. 2013. Available: http://www.victorianweb.org/authors/besant/besant2.html. *This article discusses Besant's feminist approach to topics within her Victorian culture.*

Malafaia, Teresa de Ataide. "Annie Besant's Shifting Identity and Fin-de-Siecle Culture
(3): Besant and Transgression." Online. 26 Jul. 2013. Available: http://www.victorianweb.org/authors/besant/besant3.html. *This article discusses Besant's entrance into the male world of oration and science.*

Malafaia, Teresa de Ataide. "Annie Besant's Shifting Identity and Fin-de-Siecle Culture
(4): Identity as Resistance." Online. 26 Jul. 2013. Available: http://www.victorianweb.org/authors/besant/besant4.html. *This article discusses Besant's conviction that society promotes and justifies gender differences and inequality of men and women.*

<u>BISHOP, BRIDGET</u> (1632-1692): *First woman hanged in Salem Witch Trials.*

"Bridget Bishop." Online. 30 Jul. 2013. Available: http://mayflowerfamilies.com/Salem%20Witches/bridget_bishop.htm. *This article offers background history on Bridget Bishop's life.*

"Dead, The." Online. 30 Jul. 2013. Available: www.law.umkc.edu/faculty/projects/ftrials?salem/ASAL_DE.HTM. *This article provides a sample of the death warrant and names of women who either were hanged on Gallows Hill or died in prison during the Salem Witch Trials of 1692.*

"EXAMINATION OF BRIDGET BISHOP, APRIL 19, 1692, THE." Online. 30 Jul. 2013. Available: www.law.umkc.edu/faculty/projects/ftrials/salem/ASA_BISX.HTM *This is a presentation of the court examination of accused witch, Bridget Bishop.*

"Examination of a Witch." Online. 30 Jul. 2013. Available: www.law.umkc.edu/faculty/projects/ftrials/salem/SAL_IEXA.HTM*A* *A painting, by an unnamed artist, shows a suspect forced to have her skin examined.*

"Images from the Salem Witchcraft Trials" – Bridget Bishop." Online. 30 Jul. 2013. Available: www.law.umkc.edu/faculty/projects/ftrials/salem/SAL_BBIS.HTM. *This article discusses the personal life of Bridget Bishop and how she was viewed by Salem society.*

"Images from the Salem Witchcraft Trials" – The June 10, 1692 hanging of Bridget Bishop." Online. 30 Jul. 2013. Available: www.law.umkc.edu/faculty/projects/ftrials/salem/SAL_IHAN.HTM *This is an artist's rendition of the hanging of Bridget Bishop*

"Salem Witch Trials 1692, The." Online. 30 Jul. 2013. Available: http://www.smithsonianmag.com/history-archaeology/brief-salem.html. *This is a chronology of the events that occurred during the Salem Witch Trials.*

"Salem Witch Trials Memorial." Online. 30 Jul. 2013. Available: http://www.salemweb.com/memorial/memorial.shtml. *This website provides photographs of memorial stones dedicated to the victims of the Salem Witch Trials of 1692.*

"Salem Witch Museum 1692 Tour." Online. 30 Jul. 2013. Available: http://www.salemwitchmuseum.com/tour/. *This website provides a photograph of the Bridget Bishop Home in Salem and offers a brief synopsis of events surrounding her trial and execution for practicing witchcraft.*

"Trial of Bridget Bishop, The." Online. 30 Jul. 2013. Available: http://www.ushistory.org/us/3g.asp. *This is the transcript for the trial of Bridget Bishop, who was accused of witchcraft, found guilty, and hanged in Salem in 1692.*

BLAVATSKY, HELENA (1831-1891): ***Mystic of the Theosophical Society.***

Blavatsky, Helena. "Why Do We Not Remember Our Past Lives?" The Key to Theosophy. Online. 30 Jul. 2013. Available: http://www.katinkahesselink.net/other/blavatsky-past-lives.html. *This is an online text of Blavatsky's book regarding some Theosophical beliefs regarding memory and re-incarnation.*

Goldstein, Matthew Mulligan. "Madame Blavatsky." University of Texas. Online. 30 Jul. 2013. Available: http://www.victorianweb.org/religion/blavatsky.html. *This article discusses Blavatsky's various careers and travels.*

Goldstein, Matthew Mulligan. "Theosophy and Madame Blavatsky." University of Texas. Online. 30 Jul. 2013. Available: http://www.victorianweb.org/religion/theosophy.html. *Goldstein discusses Blavatsky's work within the Theosophical Society.*

"History of the Theosophical Society. Theosophical University Press. Online. 30 Jul. 2013. Available: www.theosociety.org/pasadena/ts/tshist.htm. *This article offers a history of the Theosophical Society of which Helena Blavatsky was a famed leader.*

"H.P. Blavatsky." Online. 30 Jul. 2013. Available: www.theosociety.org/pasadena/ts/**bio**-hpb.htm. *This article contains biographical information about the life of Helena Blavatsky.*

Murphet, Howard. "When Daylight Comes: A Biography of Helena Blavatsky. The Theosophical Publishing House. 1975. *A biography of Helena Blavatsky.*

"Studies in Occultism by H.P. Blavatsky." Theosophical University Press. Online. 30 Jul. 2013. Available: http://www.theosociety.org/pasadena/hpb-sio/sio-hp.htm. *This is a brief article describing Blavatsky's book cover and her definition of the term occult.*

Van Mater, John P. "Helena Petrovna Blavatsky." Theosophical University Press. Online. 30 Jul. 2013. Available: www.theosociety.org/pasadena/sd/sd-hp.htm. *This website features a photograph of Blavatsky.*

BOSANQUET-FLETCHER, MARY (1739-1815): ***One of the first females to preach in the Methodist Church***

Bosanquet/Fletcher Letters Project. The Fletcher Page. Online. 30 Jul. 2013. Available:http://www.thefletcherpage.org/mbfletters.html. *A website dedicated to the lives, ministries, theologies, and contexts of John Fletcher and Mary Bosanquet Fletcher.*

"John Wesley: An On-Line Exhibition." John Rylands University. Online. 30 Jul. 2013. Available: rylibweb.man.ac.uk/data1/dg/methodist/jwol1.html. *This article offers copies of letters from John Wesley to Mary Bosanquet-Fletcher.*

"John and Mary Fletcher." A bibliography. Online. 30 Jul. 2013. Available: http://christianheritagefellowship.com/john-william-and-mary-fletcher-a-bib%C2%ADli%C2%ADog%C2%ADraphy/. *This online site offers a list of their publications.*

"Mary Bosanquet Fletcher." Online. 30 Jul. 2013. Available: http://gbgm-umc.org/UMW/Wesley/quiz/91.html. *This is a biographical article on Mary Bosanquet-Fletcher, Methodist preacher.*

"Mr. Wesley's Preachers." Online. 30 Jul. 2013. Available: http://gbgm-umc.org/umw/wesley/wesleywomen.stm. *This report discusses the men and women, including Mary Bosanquet Fletcher, who preached in the Methodist church under the guidance of John Wesley.*

Singleton, John. "Wesley's support boosted women preachers." United Methodist News Service.
Online. 30 Jul. 2013. Available:
http://archives.umc.org/umns/news_archive1998.asp?ptid=&story=%7B21DC1BB5-EB7B-4A1B-9AE0-2746B6BDBF30%7D&mid=3370
Singleton stresses that John Wesley was supportive of women taking active roles in the Methodist church.

BROWN, OLYMPIA (1835-1926): ***Universalist minister and suffragist.***

"Determined Reformer." Women of Courage, Ten North Country Pioneers in Profile. St. Lawrence County, NY Branch of the American Association of University Women (1989). Online. 30 Jul. 2013. Available: www.northnet.org/stlawrenceaauw./brown.htm. *This report contains biographical information on Olympia Brown.*

"Olympia Brown, Pioneer Woman Minister and Suffragette."
Online. 30 Jul. 2013. Available:
http://womenshistory.about.com/od/brownolympia/a/olympia_brown.htmT. *This website contains biographical information and a photograph of Olympia Brown.*

CLITHEROW, MARGARET (1556-1586): Catholic martyr.

Burton, Edwin. "John Mush." The Catholic Encyclopedia. Joseph P. Thomas, Trans. Online. 5 Aug. 2013. Available:
http://newadvent.org/cathen/10647c.htm.
This is a biographical article on John Mush, a priest who was Margaret Clitherow's confessor.

Camm, Bede. "St. Margaret Clitherow." The Catholic Encyclopedia. Marcia L. Bellafiore, Trans. Online. 5 Aug. 2013. Available: http://newadvent.org/cathen/04059b.htm. *This is a biographical article on the Catholic martyr, Margaret Clitherow.*

"Margaret Clitherow." Online. 5 Aug. 2013. Available: www.catholic-forum.com/sants/saintm54.htm. *This article contains biographical information on the Catholic martyr, Margaret Clitherow.*

CROSBY, FRANCES JANE (FANNY) (1820-1915): Overcame blindness to write over 5,000 Christian hymns.

"Blessed Assurance." Online. 5 Aug. 2013. Available: http://www.hymnsite.com/lyrics/umh369.sht. *This website contains the words to the Christian hymn, "Blessed Assurance," written by Fanny Crosby.*

Crosby, Fanny. An Autobiography. 1906. Eugene, Oregon: Wipf and Stock Publishers, 1986. *In this book, Frances Crosby discusses her life experiences as a blind person and as a Christian hymn writer.*

"Fanny Crosby." Online. 5 Aug. 2013. Available: www.wholesomewords.org/biography/biorpcrosby.html. *This website offers various milestones in the life of Jane Frances Crosby.*

"Frances Jane Crosby." Online. 5 Aug. 2013. Available: http://www.earnestlycontending.com/KT/bios/fannycrosby.html. *This report offers biographical information on Fanny Crosby, Christian hymn writer.*

"Frances Jane (Fanny) Crosby." Online. 5 Aug. 2013. Available: http://www.cyberhymnal.org/bio/c/r/o/crosby_fj.htm. *The report contains the titles of many of the Christian hymns Crosby wrote and the various pseudonyms she used.*

"Frances Jane "Fanny" Crosby." Online. 5 Aug. 2013. Available: www.nyise.org/fanny. " *This articles offers biographical information on Crosby.*

Johnson, Guye. "Blessed Assurance." Bob Jones University. Online. 5 Aug. 2013. Available: http://liberty-virtue-independence.blogspot.com/2011/11/phoebe-knapp-fanny-crosby.html. *This article discusses the collaboration of Frances Crosby and Phoebe Knapp in the writing of the Christian hymn, "Blessed Assurance." Their understanding of conversion expressed through their hymns.*

The New York Institute of Special Education. Online. 5 Aug. 2013. Available: www.nyise.org/fanny/styles.html. *This article discusses the way Charles Wesley and Fanny Crosby interpreted Christian conversion and expressed it in their hymns.*

DUCHESNE, ROSE PHILIPPINE (1769-1852): ***Catholic missionary to America's Western frontier.***

De Mentque, Fr. Edouard. "St. Rose Philippine Duchesne, Virgin Feast Day – November 18. Online. 5 Aug. 2013. Available: http://www.kclatinmass.com/about-st-rose-philippine-duchesne.html. *This is a biographical article on Rose Duchesne.*

"Rose Philippine Duchesne, Catholic Saint." Online. 5 Aug. 2013. Available: http://www.catholic.org/saints/saint.php?saint_id=377. *Canonization information.*

"Rose Philippine Duchesne Biography." The New York Institute of Special Education. Online. 5 Aug. 2013. Available: http://www.kshs.org/kansapedia/rose-philippine-duchesne/16877. *This biographical article tells the history of Rose Duchesne.*

"Rose Philippine Duchesne." Religious Society of the Sacred Heart. The New York Institute of Special Education. Online. 5 Aug. 2013. Available: http://www.vatican.va/news_services/liturgy/saints/ns_lit_doc_19880703_duchesne_en.html. *This is a biography of Rose Duchesne.*

DYER, MARY BARRETT (1614-1660): ***Quaker martyr.***

Behling, Sam. "Mary Barrett Dyer." Online. 5 Aug. 2013. Available: http://www.rootsweb.ancestry.com/~nwa/dyer.html. *This article describes Mary Dyer's work and death as a Quaker.*

Clark, Beth. Anne Hutchinson. Philadelphia: Chelsea House Publishers, 2000. *This book is a biographical account of the life of Anne Hutchinson and contains information on the interaction and friendship between Mary Dyer and Hutchinson.*

Plimpton, Ruth. Mary Dyer Biography of a Rebel Quaker. Boston: Branden Publishing Company, 1994. *This book provides a biographical narrative on the life of Mary Dyer, martyr for her Quaker faith.*

GRACIA, HOSOKAWA (1563-1600): ***Japanese Christian convert and martyr.***

Muromoto, Wayne. "The Tragedy of Lady Gracia." Online. 5 Aug. 2013. Available: http://fulfilledinjesus.blogspot.com/2005/07/hosokawa-gracia-1563-1600.html. *This article discusses Hosokawa Gracia's heroic but tragic life and death.*

Natori, Junichi, Life of Gracia Tama Hosokawa a Great Christian Woman in Japan, The. The Hokuseido Press. 1955. *This is a biographical book about Gracia Hosokawa.*

Prusmack, Florence. "Hosokawa Gracia." Online. 5 Aug. 2013. Available: http://www.distinguishedwomen.com/biographies/hosokawa.html. *This is a biographical article about Hosokawa Gracia.*

JONAS, REGINA (1902-1944): ***First Jewish female rabbi.***

"Family Camp Theresienstadt." Online. 5 Aug. 2013. Available: www.wsg-hist.uni-linz.ac.at/Auschwitz.html/Theresienstadt.html. *This article discusses the conditions of the German Nazi Camp to which Regina Jonas was taken during WWII.*

"First Woman Rabbi in the World, The." Online. 5 Aug. 2013. Available: http://www.hagalil.com/deutschland/berlin/rabbiner/jonas.htm. *This is a biographical account of Regina Jonas' work as a rabbi and her death in the Auschwitz concentration camp.*

Von Kellenbach, Katharina. "Rabbi Regina Jonas." St. Mary's College of Maryland. Online. 5 Aug. 2013. Available: http://faculty.smcm.edu/kvonkellenbach/reginajones.php. *This article tells of Jonas' career and accomplishments as a Jewish rabbi.*

JUDSON, ANN HASSELTINE (1789-1826): ***First American female missionary.***

"Ann Hasseltine Judson." 1998. Southern Baptist Historical Library & Archives. Online. 5 Aug. 2013. Available: www.sbhla.org/bio_annjudson.htm. *Ann Hasseltine Judson's missionary travel is discussed in this biographical sketch.*

Pitman, Emma R. Ann H. Judson of Burma. 1936. Fort Washington, Pennsylvania: Harper Collins Publishers, 1999. *This biographical book tells the story of Ann Hasseltine Judson's missionary work with her husband in Burma in the early Nineteenth Century.*

Ross, Stephen. "Ann Hasseltine Judson." Online. 5 Aug. 2013. Available: http://www.wholesomewords.org/missions/bjudsonann.html. *This is a biographical article on Ann Hasseltine Judson, the first American woman to do missionary work in a foreign country.*

Severance, Diana. "Ann Hasseltine Judson: First American Woman Missionary." Online. 5 Aug. 2013. Available: http://www.christianity.com/church/church-history/timeline/1801-1900/ann-judson-1st-american-woman-missionary-11630365.html. *The missionary work and travels of Ann Hasseltine Judson are discussed in this biographical article.*

LAVEAU, MARIE (1794-1881): ***Practiced Voodoo and Catholicism.***

"All Hail the Queen." Online. 5 Aug. 2013. Available: http://www.angelfire.com/md2/spamedham/marielav.htm. *This article discusses the apparent supernatural powers of Marie Laveau in one legendary case.*

"Bosswoman of New Orleans." Online. 5 Aug. 2013. Available: http://www.angelfire.com/md2/spamedham/marielav.htm. *This article describes the many aspects of Marie Laveau's religious work.*

"Gris-Gris." Online. 5 Aug. 2013. Available: http://www.voodoomuseum.com/index.php?option=com_content&view=article&id=15&Itemid=18. *This article discusses magic and the power of suggestion used by Marie Laveau.*

"Marie Laveau." Online. 5 Aug. 2013. Available: www.lkwdpl.org/wihohio/lave-mar.htm. *This is a brief biography of Marie Laveau.*

“Marie Laveau.” Online. 5 Aug. 2013. Available: http://www.voodoomuseum.com/index.php?option=com_content&view=article&id=15&Itemid=18. *This is a biographical article discusses Marie Laveau's great compassion for the poor.*

“Marie Laveau's Legacy.” Online. 5 Aug. 2013. Available: http://www.prairieghosts.com/laveau.html. *This article tells that Marie Laveau practiced both Voodoo and Catholicism and that her legend lives on today.*

“Marie Laveau's Tomb.” Online. 5 Aug. 2013. Available: www.yatcom.com/neworl/naborhud/treme/stlouisone/marielaveau.html. *This website offers a photograph and information regarding the burial place of Marie Laveau.*

LEE, ANN (1736-1784): *Founder of the Shaker religion.*

Campion, Nardi Reeder. Mother Ann Lee, Morning Star of the Shakers. 1976. Hanover, NH: University Press of New England, 1990. *This biographical book covers the life and times of Ann Lee, founder of the Shaker religion.*

Ewen, Julia. “The differences between being Shaker & Quaker.” Online. 5 Aug. 2013. Available: www.rootsweb.com/~quakers/shakers.htm. *This article examines the differences in the Shaker and Quaker religions.*

“Mother Ann Lee.” Online. 5 Aug. 2013. Available: www.findagrave.com/pictures/610.html. *This website offers photographs of Shaker Ann Lee's grave.*

“Mother Ann Lee (1736-1784), religious founder.” Online. 5 Aug. 2013. Available: www.cr.nps.gov/nr/travel/pwwmh/ny16.htm. *This website offers information on the Watervliet Shaker Historic District.*

“Prophecies, Visions and Revelations.” Online. 5 Aug. 2013. Available: www.passtheword.org/SHAKERMANUSCRIPTS/Testimonies/tstmnyx1.h *This website contains actual testimonies of Ann Lee and others in the Shak community.*

"Shakers, The." Online. 5 Aug. 2013. Available: http://xroads.virginia.edu/~hyper/hns/cities/shakers.html. *Both the history of the Shaker movement and community living are discussed in this article.*

<u>LUTHER, KATHARINA VON BORA</u> (1499-1555): *Wife of Martin Luther.*

"My Lord Katie: Katharina von Bora Luther." Concordia Historical Institute. Online. 5 Aug. 2013. Available: http://www.lutheranhistory.org/katie. *This website contains paintings of Katie Luther and Martin Luther, her husband.*

Scholberg, Henry. <u>Katie Luther</u>. Lima, Ohio: Fairway Press, 1993. *This one-act play is based on the life of Katharina Von Bora Luther, the wife of Martin Luther.*

Stjerna, Kirsi. "Pioneer Woman of the Reformation." Online. 5 Aug. 2013. Available: http://www.thelutheran.org/article/article.cfm?article_id=646. *This biographical article marks the 500th anniversary of Katie Luther's birth.*

<u>McPHERSON, AIMEE SEMPLE</u> (1890-1944): *Pentecostal evangelist.*

"A Woman of Destiny." Online. 5 Aug. 2013. Available: http://www.godsgenerals.com/person_a_mcpherson.htm. *This is a biographical article on Aimee Semple McPherson.*

Epstein, Daniel Mark. Sister Aimee, <u>The Life of Aimee Semple McPherson</u>. New York: Harcourt Brace & Company, 1993. Epstein's book covers Aimee Semple McPherson's life from her birth in 1890 through her colorful and fascinating life as an evangelist and faith healer.

"Foursquare Gospel, The." 12 Mar. 1939. Online. 5 Aug. 2013. Available: http://www.foursquare.org/about/history. *This is a biography of Aimee Semple McPherson, evangelist.*

Greenstein, Albert. "Aimee Semple McPherson." 1999. Online. 5 Aug. 2013. Available: http://www.worldcat.org/title/aimee-semple-mcpherson/oclc/45389179. *This article offers biographical information on Aimee Semple McPherson.*

"Kidnapping of Aimee Semple McPherson, The." Online. 5 Aug. 2013. Available: http://www.usc.edu/libraries/archives/la/scandals/aimee.html. *This article discusses the belief of many that Aimee Semple McPherson's kidnapping w a hoax.*

<u>MURRAY, GRACE</u> (1738-1803): *Methodist leader.*

Daugherty, Ruth. "Grace Murray." Online. 5 Aug. 2013. Available: http://gbgm-umc.org/umw/wesley/gracemurray.stm. *This is a brief article regarding the relationship between Grace Murray and John Wesley.*

"John Wesley: Christian Perfection." Online. 5 Aug. 2013. Available: http://www.theologian-theology.com/theologians/john-wesley-christian-perfection. *The article states that John Wesley bought an old foundry in which he organized The Methodist Society.*

Wakeley, J.B. "John Wesley and Grace Murray." Anecdotes of the Wesley's: Illustrative of Their Character and Personal History. New York: Nelson & Phillips, 1869. Online. 5 Aug. 2013. Available: http://archive.org/details/anecdotesofwesle00wake. *Wakeley discusses John Wesley's love for Grace Murray.*

<u>SETON, ELIZABETH</u> (1774-1821): *Founder of the Sisters of Charity.*

"Biography of St. Elizabeth Ann Seton." The National Shrine of Saint Elizabeth Ann Seton. 1995. Online 5 Aug. 2013. Available: http://www.setonheritage.org/education/biography-of-st-elizabeth-ann-seto *This is a biographical article on Elizabeth Seton.*

"Elizabeth Bayley Seton 1774-1821." Online. 5 Aug. 2013. Available: www.greatwomen.org/seton.htm. This *is a biographical article on Elizabet Seton, educator and Catholic saint.*

Grunwell, Jeanne Marie. <u>Saint Elizabeth Ann Seton</u>. Boston: Pauline Books & Media, 1999. This *book is a biographical account of the life of Elizabeth Seton, Sisters of Charity and Roman Catholic parochial education in the U founder.*

"Seton, Saint Elizabeth Ann." Catholic Life Online. Online. 5 Aug. 2013. Available: http://www.catholic.org/saints/saint.php?saint_id=180. *This is a biographical article on Elizabeth Seton.*

__SNOW, ELIZA__ **(1804-1887):** ***Mormon wife and poet.***

Bachman, Daniel and Ronald K. Esplin. "History of Plural Marriage." Online. 5 Aug. 2013. Available: http://www.lightplanet.com/mormons/daily/history/plural_marriage/polygamy_history.html. *This article offers a history of Mormon polygamy in the 19th Century.*

"Eliza Roxcy Snow." Mormon Literature – Who's Who. Online. 5 Aug. 2013. Available: http://mormonlit.lib.byu.edu/lit_author.php?a_id=562. *This article provides biographical information on Eliza Snow, Mormon poet.*

Leonard, Glen M. __Nauvoo: A Place of Peace, a People of Promise__ Deseret Book Co. June 2002. *This book provides historical information regarding the city in Illinois where exiled Mormons lived until they were driven out by their persecutors.*

Smith, Barbara B. and Shirley W. Thomas. "Roles of LDS Women." Online. 5 Aug. 2013. Available: http://www.lightplanet.com/family/mothers/women_roles.html. *The online article explains the functions and lives of women in the Latter-day Saints community.*

Mormonism. Online. 5 Aug. 2013. Available: http://www.religionfacts.com/mormonism/index.htm. *This article answers questions about the Mormon religion and culture.*

"Wives of Joseph Smith, The." Online. 5 Aug. 2013. Available: http://www.wivesofjosephsmith.org/15-ElizaRSnow.htm. *This site provides historical background on Eliza Snow's life.*

__TEKAKWITHA, KATERI__ **(1656-1680):** ***Mohawk convert to Christianity.***

"Blessed Kateri Tekakwitha." Online. 6 Aug. 2013. Available: www.catholic.org/saints/saints/kateritekakwitha.html. This *article provides background information on the Mohawk Christian, Kateri Tekakwitha.*

"Blessed Kateri Tekakwitha." Online. 6 Aug. 2013. Available: http://www.pitt.edu/~eflst4/Kateri.html. *This is a brief biographical article on the Mohawk Christian, Kateri Tekakwitha.*

"Blessed Kateri Tekakwitha Honoring Page." Online. 6 Aug. 2013. Available: http://pweb.netcom.com/~rnroybal/kateri.html. This *website provides links to information on the Mohawk Christian, Kateri Tekakwitha, and an artist's rendition of her.*

Bunson, Margaret R. Kateri Tekakwitha, Mystic of the Wilderness. Huntington, Indiana: Our Sunday Visitor Publishing Division, 1992. This *book provides an in-depth study of the life of Kateri Tekakwitha, the Mohawk woman who converted to Catholicism.*

Hassenplug, Sarah. "Highlights of the Life of Blessed Kateri Tekakwitha." Online. 6 Aug. 2013. Available: http://www.cin.org/kat8.html. *This biographical article discusses false accusations against Kateri Tekakwitha.*

Kelly, Blanche M. "Blessed Kateri Tekakwitha." The Catholic Encyclopedia. 1999. Online. 6 Aug. 2013. Available: http://www.newadvent.org/cathen/14471a.htm. This *is a biographical artic*[illegible] *on Kateri Tekakwitha.*

"Lily of the Mohawks." Online. 6 Aug. 2013. Available: http://www.lily-of-the-mohawks.com. *This is a biographical account of Kateri Tekakwitha's life.*

Mitchell, Kateri. "Biographical Sketch of blessed Kateri Tekakwitha." 1 Sep. 1996. Online. 6 Aug. 2013. Available: www.cin.org/kat7.html. This *is a biographical account of Kateri Tekakwitha's life.*

Providencia, Sr. "A Reflection on Kateri's Influence." Online. 6 Aug. 2013. Available: www.cin.org/kat9.html. This *is a brief commentary regarding Kateri Tekakwitha's religious influence on Indian tribes of the far west.*

Raymond, John. "Blessed Kateri Tekakwitha." 12 Jul. 1998. Online. 6 Aug. 2013. Available: www.monksofadoration.org/Kateri.html. This *article gives biographical information on Kateri Tekakwitha.*

Savilla, Edmund. "The Prophetic Spirit of Kateri Tekakwitha Within Our Indian Churches." 1 Sep. 1996. Online. 6 Aug. 2013. Available: www.cin.org/kat10.html. This *is a Catholic priest's version of the Christia*[illegible] *colonization of the Mohawk Indians by the Jesuits.*

Skanaieah, Sarah. "Blessed Kateri Tekakwitha, Lily of the Mohawks." Online. 6 Aug. 2013. Available: http://www.blessedkateriparish.org/Blessed%20Kateri.html. *The events of Tekakwitha's life are listed in this report.*

White, Julia. "Kateri Tekakwitha (Lily of the Mohawks) – Mohawk." Online. 6 Aug. 2013. Available: www.powersource.com/gallery/womansp/mohawk.html. *Self- mutilation and self-induced physical tortures are discussed in this biographical article on Kateri Tekakwitha.*

WESLEY, SUSANNA (1669-1742): ***Mother of John and Charles Wesley, Methodist founders.***

Pellow, Susan. Susanna Wesley's Biography. Online. 6 Aug. 2013. Available: http://susanpellowe.com/susanna-wesley.htm. This *is a biographical article on Susanna Wesley, mother of John and Charles Wesley, founders of Methodism.*

McReynolds, Kathy. Susanna Wesley. Minneapolis, Minnesota: Bethany House Publishers, 1998. This *book offers a biographical account of Susanna Wesley's life as the mother of nineteen children and, in particular, as the mother of John and Charles Wesley who became the founders of Methodism.*

Wakeley, J.B. "Susanna Wesley and the Unauthorized Meetings." Online. 6 Aug. 2013. Available: http://gbgm-umc.org/umw/wesley/susannawesley.stm. *The article discusses the meetings she held in opposition to her church.*

WILKINSON, JEMIMA (1752-1819): ***Founder of a religious order, "The Universal Friends."***

Brekus, Catherine. Strangers and Pilgrims: Female Preaching in America, 1740-1845. University of North Carolina Press, The. *The book presents biographical information on Jemima Wilkinson, religious founder, her preaching and other female preachers.*

Henretta, James. "Unruly Women: Jemima Wilkinson and Deborah Sampson Gannett." The Early America Review (Fall 1996): 3 pp. Online. 6 Aug. 2013. Available: http://www.earlyamerica.com/review/fall96/biography.html. *The article describes the controversial actions of Jemima Wilkinson and Deborah Sampson Gannett.*

"Jemima Wilkinson House." 30 Mar. 1998. Online. 6 Aug. 2013. Available: www.cr.nps.gov/nr/travel/pwwmh/ny7.htm. *Jemima Wilkinson's religious affiliations and photos of her home and surrounding area are featured in this article.*

Wilkinson, Jill. "Jemima Wilkinson." Online. 6 Aug. 2013. Available: http://www.rootsweb.ancestry.com/~nwa/jemima.html. *This article provide family history and background for Jemima Wilkinson, founder of a religiou order called "The Universal Friends.*

<u>WILLARD, FRANCES</u> (1839-1898): *Christian Temperance Union leader.*

"Frances Willard and the Women's Christian Temperance Union, 1874-1898." Online. 6 Aug. 2013. Available: http://www.franceswillardhouse.org/uploads/HST391-Project-2-finished_-_printer.pdf. *Prohibition and the Christian Women's Temperance movemen are discussed in this article.*

"Temperance Movement." <u>Compton's Encyclopedia Online</u>. Online. 6 Aug. 2013. Available: http://www.encyclopedia.com/topic/temperance_movements.aspx. *This article contains information on the Christian Women's Temperance movement.*

"Willard, Frances." <u>Encyclopedia.com</u>. Online. 6 Aug. 2013. Available: http://www.encyclopedia.com/topic/Frances_Elizabeth_Willard.aspx. This *is a brief biographical article on Frances Willard, leader of the Christian Women's Temperance movement.*

Willard, Frances E. <u>A Wheel Within A Wheel</u>. 1895. Bedford, Massachusetts: Applewood Books, 1999. *In her book, Frances Willard describes how she, fifty-three years of age, learned to ride a bike, using her experience to poin out that goals may be accomplished through tenacity.*

"Women's Christian Temperance Union, The ." Online. 6 Aug. 2013. Available: http://www.google.com/search?q=Women's+Christian+Temperance+Unio &tbm=isch&tbo=u&source=univ&sa=X&ei=ORABUpLqOKbmyQGk0oC Cg&ved =0CEwQsAQ&biw=985&bih=728. *This historical site provides photos of the women in the Women's Christian Temperance Union.*

Ordering Books

U.S. 12.95 + 3.50 Shipping

CANADA 14.95 + Shipping (Request Quote)

PayPal orders accepted to:
Coralie Johnson
cjohnson@umich.edu

or

Send Check or MO to:

Wildwood Press
1112 S. Durand St.
Jackson, MI 49203

Group discounts available